Fr. Jeffrey Kirby

REAL RELIGION

HOW TO AVOID FALSE FAITH AND WORSHIP GOD IN SPIRIT AND TRUTH

Catholic
Answers
Press

Published by Catholic Answers, Inc.
2020 Gillespie Way
El Cajon, California 92020
1-888-291-8000 orders
619-387-0042 fax
catholic.com

Printed in the United States of America
Cover by Claudine Mansour Design
Interior by Russell Graphic Design

978-1-68357-231-2
978-1-68357-232-9 Kindle
978-1-68357-233-6 ePub

REAL RELIGION

HOW TO AVOID FALSE FAITH AND WORSHIP GOD IN SPIRIT AND TRUTH

To
Aaron J. Kirby
State Trooper and Nephew

CONTENTS

INTRODUCTION

Throughout my priesthood, I have always labored to be as available as possible to anyone who wants to meet. Because of this open interaction, I've had some edifying and encouraging conversations, as well as some distressing and disturbing ones. It's amazing to hear what's happening in the trenches of our faith.

On one such occasion, a younger couple asked to meet and discuss the Mass and Catholic worship in general. I was elated by their interest and looked forward to the conversation. But we had barely started when the couple began to criticize the order of the Mass, its repetition and sobriety, the choice of music, the absence of a "welcoming spirit," the somber tone, the lack of energy, and the bad homilies. In contrast, they asked for engaging music, more fellowship, an upbeat tone, homilies with stories and nuanced styles, and more interaction. In summary, they wanted the Catholic Mass to resemble the worship service of a megachurch.

Oddly, of the many things that were mentioned, there was a notable oversight. After the couple had explained and offered suggestions for almost an hour, I just looked at them and asked, "But where's God?"

There was an understandable pause, and then secondary attempts to explain how their ideas would help us get closer to God. But even their explanations were lacking in terms of true worship. So I said, "It seems that all these suggestions would engage us, inspire us, and entertain us. But where is the worship of God? Shouldn't our liturgy help us to quiet down, refocus our minds and hearts, and then lead us to encounter and adore God?"

The couple were frustrated and told me I was taking their thoughts out of context, and so I asked them to help me understand. I pointed out that I had just listened to them for almost an hour, and not even the word "God" was spoken.

"Do you think it says something," I asked, "that we had an entire conversation on worship, and God's name was not even spoken? Could that possibly tell us something about the ideas themselves or the spirit behind them?"

"But Father, if you do these types of things, people will come!"

"Okay, but come to what? Our work is not simply to amass a large group of people."

"But Father, don't you want more people to come?"

"Yes, of course, but that is not the goal of worship. Worship is the adoration offered to God by his chosen people on his terms. Worship is not the Church's principal outlet for evangelization. We don't adjust our worship so that more people might attend. We worship so as to praise and glorify God, not our own hearts, or our own community, or even our own desire for a large group."

Needless to say, the young couple left my office bewildered. Our conversation turned their world upside-down. Regrettably, I think it was the first time that worship, born from the revelation of God and from his clear directions on how to worship him, were presented to these younger Christians.

The standard of all things

In light of Western culture's modern submergence into subjectivism and relativism, such self-focused views of worship shouldn't be surprising. They still are, especially among baptized Christians, but the cultural landscape provides a broad context in which to evaluate and dissect these peculiar liturgical views.

Modern Western culture, separated from the convictions that created it, has convinced people that they are the standard of all things. The lie is propagated: something has value only because I find it subjectively satisfying. My emotions are the end-all and be-all of everything, even the worship of God.

The gas we breathe

In absolutizing our emotions and ways of thinking, we perpetuate the sin of our first parents and display the consequences of our fallen state. Even as God blessed Adam and Eve with sanctifying grace and guided them on the proper way of life, he respected their freedom and gave them a means to reciprocate or refuse his love.

The Genesis account describes God's instruction not to eat of the Tree of the Knowledge of Good and Evil. The tree was not merely a tree of general knowledge. Adam and Eve were free and knew good from evil. This tree was the ultimate fodder for temptation (and deception): Satan could falsely claim that it gave a knowledge that does not *discern*, but rather *decides and determines* what is good and what is evil. For Adam and Eve to accept such a temptation was to attempt to seize divine power. It was a concerted effort to steal the majesty of God for themselves.

In refusing to reciprocate God's love, our first parents chose themselves over God. They chose lies over truth, deception over transparency, and pleasure over virtue. Adam and Eve rebelled against worship and sought to declare themselves gods. They desired to worship only themselves.

This act of rebellion by the first human beings caused harm to our human nature and to the created world. All created existence fell from grace. Our bodies now suffer corruptibility, our intellects are darkened, our memories are blurred, our passions wage war against themselves, and we have lost the beauty of dwelling in God's presence.

All of this fallen reality is played out in a thousand different ways every day. It is particularly displayed in humanity's constant revolt against true worship of God and our perpetual drive to worship ourselves.

In his usual satirical way, the novelist Mark Twain summarized this tension, saying: "God made man in his own image, and man is forever trying to repay the favor."

In this overthrow of reality, we place the epistemological over the metaphysical, our emotional intelligence over rational intelligence and reasoned thought. We falsely believe that whatever we might think or feel is somehow equal to or greater than what something truly is. We forget that there is an objective order outside our limited minds and beyond the arena of our emotions. In such confusion, true worship is lost and seductively replaced by communitarianism, euphoria, and other forms of self-worship.

Such narcissism is so imbedded into our fallen nature that even the best among us struggle to identify and overcome it. It is a part of what author Flannery O'Connor described as "the gas we breathe."

The "happy child list"

As an example of this man-made, man-focused false worship, I'm reminded of another story from my priestly ministry.

Every year, there is a battle over First Holy Communion. Suddenly, a small army of children show up. They were baptized but never raised or formed in the Faith. Now the parents and the family want the child to receive more sacraments of a God they do not know. As the parish seeks to use the situation as an opportunity to introduce the child and family back into the regular and devout practice of the Faith, the family play games. They skip classes, leave retreats early, have multiple "illnesses," favor sports in scheduling conflicts, and do only what is absolutely required in order to receive the sacraments.

Parish catechetical staff are exhausted as they try to keep up with and track such a family. For such families, worship is solely about getting something and marking some rite of passage in the lives of their children.

On one such occasion, a set of parents were upset because the parish recommended a year delay in their child's reception of Holy Communion. The suggestion was made in good faith and with a sincere care for the authentic spiritual development of the child. The idea was not received well, and the parents insisted on seeing me.

The meeting started coldly. I asked them to explain their understanding of the suggestion. It was laced with unfounded criticism, harsh exaggerations of the people involved, and a tangible self-righteousness, summarized by the assertion: "Who do you think you people are to refuse my child Communion?"

The conversation continued:

"No one is refusing Holy Communion to anyone. We're suggesting another year of formation so your child will be more readily disposed to receive the graces of the sacrament. I'm sure you're aware of how many portions of the program your child missed this past year."

"There were a lot of family issues. We don't need to explain those. Our child is ready and should be able to receive Communion with her class."

"Yes, you don't have to explain any absences, if they're related to family issues. But the reasons for the absences are only one part of this situation. The other part is that your child didn't receive a full year's worth of formation. She's not ready, and I want you to see that our request is based on a desire for your child to fully know what's happening and to be ready to develop a deeper relationship with Jesus Christ."

"We don't understand why our child is being singled out. She's in the second grade. It's time for her to receive Communion."

"Well, your family is not the only one to receive this request. But, okay, your child is in the second grade. It sounds as though my points about spiritual preparation aren't being received. Don't you want your child to know and love Jesus Christ? There must be some reason why you're pushing the reception of the sacrament."

"Father, we just want our child to receive Communion. We are doing our best to give her a happy childhood. We don't understand why this is such a big deal."

Wow! There it was. The conversation concluded. It didn't end well in terms of human respect, but it ended superbly in terms of divine worship. It was tragically clear that the sacrament as worship and divine communion meant nothing. It was just one expectation that the parents had given themselves to provide their daughter with a happy childhood. The sacrament was right up there with meeting Santa Claus, going to Disney World, and making an overseas trip. It was only about the pictures, the white dress, the fancy rosary beads, and the family party.

Whereas such attentiveness of the parents is praiseworthy in a general sense of life, it is misplaced and lacking a proper sense of religion when applied to a sacrament. This is another example of worship being disordered and turned into something other than what it's called to be.

The love God has for us

In spite of our efforts to minimize the reality of God, and to compromise our call to love and worship him, God remains infinitely perfect and ever steadfast. In spite of our sinfulness, he continuously calls us to himself.

Once, while St. Teresa of Ávila was in prayer, the Lord Jesus appeared to her and asked her who she was. The saint replied with her religious name: "I am Teresa of Jesus." The Lord smiled, and when the saint asked him who he was, he replied to her, "I am Jesus of Teresa." The story illustrates the intimacy that Jesus Christ desires to have with each of us. It is the purpose behind his summons for us to worship him, since it places us in our proper context in creation and allows us to prosper as human beings who were made and designed to worship.

As St. Paul teaches us:

We know that all things work together for good with those who love him, who are called according to his purpose (Rom. 8:28).

Further, the apostle explains:

When all things are subjected to him, then the Son himself will also be subjected to him who put all things under him, that God may be everything to every one (1 Cor. 15:28).

And so, God gives us the true standard. He offers us the invitation to reciprocate his love. The life that God beckons us to live on this earth is the life we need in order to flourish as human beings and so fulfill our purpose and share in his eternal life.

Why this book?

This book is written out of a desire to remind us all of God's everlasting love for us and our capacity to love him back through *right and real religion*. From countless conversations and experiences, it has become tragically clear to me that there is a pressing pastoral need to address what worship is, how it has been revealed by God, and how it has been historically expressed in the revered virtue of religion. This book will cover these themes.

Chapter one covers the virtue of religion and the basic tenets of biblical worship. The historical development of revealed religion is given, especially in terms of its connection to divinely given worship and the perpetual threat of idolatry. This chapter is used as a foundation for all of the remaining chapters of the book.

Chapter two begins a four-part exploration into some of the principal modern threats to revealed religion. The first such threat is when religion becomes a sentiment. The emotionalization of society and the masquerading of mere sentiment as religion will be thoroughly explored in light of the tenets of chapter one. The connection between relativism and personal emotions is researched, especially as they lead to the danger of self-worship.

Chapter three evaluates when religion becomes self-help. The cultural phenomenon of self-help is evaluated, and the "best version" fallacy is dissected. The proper rapport between worship and our way of life will be provided. The proper boundaries of psychology are explained, and the subordination of healing to worship is argued.

Chapter four dives into the problem of religion becoming a commodity. The commercialization of religion, the gimmicks found in man-made worship, and the "shopping around" mentality are unmasked as an affront to true, biblical worship and the authentic virtue of religion.

Chapter five exposes when religion becomes social activism. The place of social activism, and how it is meant to assist with proper worship, is developed. The threat of removing substance from worship and social outreach, and of keeping only the externals without an obedience of faith and a desire for internal conversion, is unveiled as a serious menace to true religion.

The book concludes with a review of our call to worship God in spirit and truth.

The structure of this book

After chapter one, each chapter provides teachings on a false form of worship. It compares the false worship against the marks of authentic religion.

After the teachings are provided in the chapter, a section entitled *Application to Our Lives* is provided. This section contains the following:

Quotes
Each chapter gives two to three quotes relating to the chapter's contents from saints or recognized holy people in the Christian tradition.

Examination of conscience
Each chapter provides a series of penetrating questions meant to help the reader identify aspects of the respective form of false worship in his own heart and in our society.

Pointers for apologetics
The chapter contains a list of steps to assist the reader in helping others to identify the errors of the respective area of false worship.

Key points
Each chapter provides a list of key points for the reader.

Devotional exercise
The chapter gives a proposed prayer or devotion to assist the reader in keeping the respective form of false worship away from his own heart and home.

Let's begin!
With the struggle of man-made worship before us, and a man-focused religion rampant in our society, we are in great need of a thorough study of the virtue of religion and of a dynamic flourishing of biblical worship in our world today.

It is my hope that this book will contribute to this overall mission, and that it might assist you in some way to bring about true religion and worship in your own heart and home.

And so, let's begin! We pray:

> But I through the abundance of thy steadfast love
> will enter thy house,
> I will worship toward thy holy temple
> in the fear of thee.
> Lead me, O Lord, in thy righteousness
> because of my enemies;
> make thy way straight before me.
> —Ps. 5:7–8

And now, let's start with chapter one and the biblical criteria of worship and religion.

1

THE TENETS OF BIBLICAL RELIGION

Some years ago, while visiting another parish, I was vested and waiting in the narthex to start Mass. With me in the narthex were the altar servers, the sacristan, and an usher. Out of the blue, one of the teenage altar servers approached me and said, "Father, I'm not ready. I don't think I can receive Holy Communion today. I think I need to go to confession."

Well, the comment sent a wave of discomfort throughout the entire narthex. What was this kid saying?

After he was done, I calmly replied, "Okay, well, we're about the start Mass right now. And so, for today, just ask for a blessing. And then confession can be available after Mass, or you can come at one of the regular times later. Sound good?"

The young man agreed and went back in line. Shortly afterward, the opening hymn started, and we processed in for worship.

Now, certainly, the young Christian will need to learn some discretion, but what a powerful example of recognizing the dignity of true worship. Perhaps without even realizing it, he was acknowledging that the standards of worship are something beyond himself, beyond his own emotions, beyond his own comfort, and beyond even the state of his own soul. He recognized that worship is something we are all called to prepare for, adjust to, and accept on its own terms. Worship is about God. Our participation in worship is a part of the virtue of religion. The young man in this story realized this truth and lived it. Do we?

Our understanding of worship is grounded upon our views of God, the virtue of religion, our duties and responsibilities before God, the biblical history and marks of true religion, and the threats to authentic religion in our modern world.

This chapter will explore each of these areas. It will particularly highlight the five basic standards of the virtue of religion. These standards will be used in the following chapters of the book as a help in assessing various forms of false worship and religion.

God Is Real

We begin with the simple assertion: God is real. Another story might help us to realize the eminence but also the nuance of this statement.

When I was in the seminary at the Pontifical North American College in Rome, one of my apostolates was to give English-speaking tours of St. Peter's Basilica. In such a role, I encountered people of every sort and kind. Every week, parts of the world passed through my tour of the basilica.

In my tour, since we were on "home turf," I attempted to give a full summary of the Christian faith through the architecture, art, monuments, and history of this universally esteemed and recognized house of worship.

If a tour was going particularly well and the people were interested and engaged, then I would add a few parts. One of those extras was the Altar of the Lie. This is the altar immediately across from the entrance to the sacristy. The altar depicts the death of Ananias and Sapphira (Acts 5:1–11). It was placed near the sacristy, where priests would prepare for worship, so that as the priest left the sacristy to go to an altar to offer Mass, he would see it and be reminded of his call to have a purity of intention while offering the sacrifice.

On one occasion, I took a very interactive tour group to this altar. While in front of the massive and beautiful mosaic of the scene, I recounted the incident from the Acts of the Apostles: a husband and wife separately lied to the apostles about money received from a sale of land, and both were struck dead for their deception. The story greatly disturbed one woman listening. She shook her head and blurted out, "God wouldn't do that."

The interruption caught me off guard, but I smiled gently and tried to clarify. "Yes, I know it can be a surprise when we see God exercise justice."

The woman was unrelenting and retorted, "God wouldn't do that. He's not like that."

I then assumed a lack of knowledge and followed up with, "Well, ma'am, the Acts of the Apostles is a part of the New Testament, which is a part of the Bible. It's through the Bible that we truly know who God is."

Her reply shouldn't have shocked me, but it did: "Well, my God wouldn't do that. He's a God of mercy."

Regrettably, due to the nature of a tour, I wasn't able to give more of a reply at the time. I offered to speak with the woman afterward, but she disappeared.

I give this story here because the woman was expressing a particular point but also a general one. The specific point is whether God would exercise justice in this way. The broader point is how we can know God and how God has spoken to us of himself and whether we will accept this revelation. It is this broader point that I want to stress here.

God is real. Divine revelation is God's self-initiated disclosure of his own knowledge of himself to the human family. This disclosure is an unveiling of himself. In modern terms, we would say his revelation is an intimate sharing of himself with humanity. Due to our fallen nature, which is inclined to the influence of sin and error, the broad knowledge we have of God through the natural light of reason depends upon God's supernatural revelation. It is God's supernatural revelation that provides for us the interior knowledge of himself that is above reason and which we could have only as a gift from him. And so, our sure knowledge of God hinges upon and comes from God's revelation.

Under the guidance of the Holy Spirit, God's revelation is contained in Sacred Tradition and Sacred Scripture. It is authentically interpreted and applied to modern life by the ordained shepherds chosen by God.

If we attempt to portray God in opposition to his revelation, we are creating an idol. If we adjust his revelation or attempt an "upgrade" by modern standards, we are fashioning our own deity. If we rely on our emotional needs or worldly, fallen perceptions of virtue in approaching God, then we are worshipping only projections of ourselves. These are all offensive to true revelation since they dismiss the identity of the true God and replace him with what we think he should be. The standard is backward; the approach is upside-down; the result is idolatrous and tragic.

In the story above, the woman had fashioned her own idol. Even when revelation called her to re-evaluate her views, and to wrestle with and accept the gift of sure knowledge of who God is, she declined and chose instead to create her own god. She chose to worship her own creation rather than her true Creator. Sadly, in this way, she is a sign of our age.

How are we to understand revelation? How can it lead us to a true knowledge and worship of the living God?

Build your own deity?

The *Catechism of the Catholic Church* (CCC) begins by teaching: "God, infinitely perfect and blessed in himself, in a plan of sheer goodness freely created man to make him share in his own blessed life" (1). It is an uplifting thought that the first word of the *Catechism* is "God" and that the *Catechism*'s first entry emphasizes his perfection.

It is ironic that what would seem to be an obvious observation is now a countercultural declaration—namely, that God is perfect. In truth, he is infinitely perfect. He doesn't need a reboot, an upgrade, or any assistance from any of his creatures to be somehow better or more relevant, or more kind, or more merciful. God is infinitely perfect. He doesn't need our help to make him any better.

Within his perfection, he is blessed in himself. He's not looking for any affirmation from us. He doesn't need our praise or adoration. He doesn't rely on our fellowship. His perfection or blessedness is not diminished because we turn from him or create our own idols. As the Holy Trinity—Father, Son, and Holy Spirit—God is a divine family and shares love and blessedness within himself. He created us in an act of sheer goodness. He wants to share with us what he already possesses within himself. He invites us to love and praise him because these build us up and make us more ourselves.

In receiving God's revelation of himself, therefore, we must remind ourselves of these basic truths and accept them in our own hearts. As fallen human beings, we should hold a healthy suspicion of ourselves so we don't re-create God according to our own desires, or our own worldview, or our own capacity to fully understand him. Our task is not to change God, but to allow the living God to change us, and to convert our hearts to love him and worship him more faithfully.

As a help, we can draw a lighter observation from popular culture. Some time ago, in many malls throughout the United States, there were certain stores where children could go and build their own stuffed animal. Having taken nieces and nephews to such places, it was always comical to see what they would come up with. The store had every possible option a child could imagine. He was free to create whatever he wanted. And so, visits to such places were an entertaining experience and a wonderful place for children.

We can apply the same concept to modern neo-idolatry. Many people approach God with almost a kind of "build your own deity" mentality. The modern person, lost in his own mind and believing that his heart is the only standard of reality, designs his own god. He spawns his own higher power and projects himself (and his fallenness) on his pseudo-deity. Such a person ends up worshipping only himself.

In this idolatrous action, a person finds himself far from the true God. If he wants to know the living God, he must abandon his idols, convict his fallen heart, and turn to the revelation given by the God of Abraham.

More than Torah?

While participating in a conference on interreligious dialogue, a rabbi introduced a maxim to the group. It was confusing when we first heard it. The simple statement was, "If you love God more than Torah, then it is not God that you love." The expression needed some explaining since, when it's first heard, it might seem backward to modern thinking.

Placed within the context of the reality of God and his revelation, the expression is rightside-up. In the Jewish tradition, as well as in the Christian tradition, we can authentically know God only through divinely confirmed natural revelation and direct, supernatural revelation. And we can love only what we know. God, therefore, is loved through the knowledge we receive through revelation. If we claim to love "God" more than his revelation, then we are not worshipping the true God. We are loving something other than the true God, since the living God can truly be known, loved, and worshipped only through his own self-disclosure to us.

The expression reflects the paradoxical method of rabbinical teaching and should not be overthought. Its approach is meant to shake the student and press a point into his mind and heart. With this maxim, we have to be cautious that God's revelation remains a gift and a means to know and love him. We have to be attentive that the sources of revelation, such as the Bible, do not themselves become idols. The revelation is necessary, but it remains a means to God himself.

God in a box

The necessity of revelation and of knowing God on his terms is not accepted in our culture today. A story can help illustrate this tension.

In our society, for decades bumper stickers have been used as a means of self-declaration. Beyond the popular Christian "fish" bumper sticker, and the reactionary Darwin one, we find all kinds of political, social, and religious statements on the bumpers of people's cars. They were our original social media "walls" before the internet existed, and even today they can incite as much of a response as a comment on Twitter.

With that in mind, I recently saw a bumper sticker that asserted: "You can't keep God in your box." As a Catholic Christian who acknowledges God's true presence in the Eucharist, which is reserved in the tabernacle (a type of box) in every Catholic Church, I found the sticker comical at first. Of course, protecting and reserving God in his tabernacle is not the point of the statement. If only we were in a culture where the Lord's presence in the Eucharist were a topic of popular discussion and debate!

No, the bumper sticker was one more version of the popular "co-exist" sticker. The statement is a reaction against organized religion and creedal belief in God. In our context, it was a response against God's revelation, especially when accepted and asserted as the true and only means to know God.

The full cultural argument goes something like this: religion isn't necessary. God is whatever you want him to be. You can believe whatever you want. Your religion is for you. No one has any higher claim on a knowledge of God. Don't be a jerk and tell me what to believe. Co-exist and be happy. Live and let live (unless you're an unborn child).

In essence, our fallen world tells us we can "build our own deity." Such a false freedom also declares that none of this is real. God is not real. It's all about us and what we want. It's about our emotional fulfillment.

In response to such intoxicating views, we speak wisdom, and so we offer these thoughts:

- First, God is real. He is infinitely perfect and blessed in himself. This is a statement of reality, not my own personal preference.

- Second, it is true: no one can keep God in his own box.

- Third, God—in an act of sheer goodness—has placed himself within *God's* own "box"—namely, his own revelation. He has spoken to us about himself and has shared his own knowledge of himself with the human family.

- Fourth, we are called to share this amazing act of love with all men and women that they might know God, living and true, and come to accept his love and mercy.

- Fifth, we speak this truth in love. We recognize and will defend a person's freedom from coercion into the Faith, even when he declines or mocks our efforts to share God's revelation.

God has revealed himself to us. By acknowledging this revelation, we are not placing God in a box. Rather, we are accepting his invitation to meet him in his own box, which is infinite, far beyond the depths of the oceans and far above the heights of the skies. We meet the true God on his terms and come to know him by his own self-disclosure.

God is perfect, blessed, and a divine family. He is not a psychological consolation, a lucky charm, or a cherished family heirloom. He is living and true. And he calls us to know him, love him, and worship him.

Do we accept God's revelation in our own lives? Do we accept him on his own terms and seek to faithfully follow and worship him?

Our Duty to God

Earlier in my priesthood, I served as the vicar of vocations for my diocese, working extensively with young adults. In this way, I came to have a deep appreciation for the younger generation. Even as they struggled with entitlement, loss of purpose, and other such things, they also showed a genuine love for and desire to serve others, especially the suffering.

In particular, what stood out for me was the deep esteem that those younger people had for their grandparents. They enjoyed being with them, hearing their stories, and witnessing their way of life, and they relished the older generation's stability. And they had a greater spiritual connection with their grandparents than with their parents. They saw their parents' generation as inconsistent and unreliable. It was their parents' generation that introduced them to no-fault divorce, legalized abortion, and other laws and cultural behaviors that imploded the stability of marriage and dis-integrated their families. In reaction, young people turned to their grandparents, appreciating their faith, wisdom, and sense of commitment.

In case of point, a young university student told me a story that stands out in my mind. It's a story that can help us address our duty to God. The young man explained to me that he was very close to his grandfather. The older man was a veteran from the Korean War. He retired as a business-man and spent his retirement serving his community and his extended family, including this grandson.

The young man described his grandfather in glowing terms. The older man woke up early, prepared breakfast for his wife, went to daily Mass, took a walk in the park (where he knew everyone there), did some woodworking, watched old Western television shows, volunteered at the local soup kitchen, and the list goes on. He was a happy man, comfort-able in his own skin and satisfied with life.

On regular visits, this young man would tag along with his grandfather. When they went to daily Mass, the older man always served. On one occasion, the young man told his grandfather, "I think you're the oldest altar boy in the Church!" They both laughed. But the grandson continued, "Grandpa, why do you go to Mass every day? Isn't Sunday enough? The Mass is really early." His grandfather smiled and told him, "I go to Mass because it's what men do."

The young man was surprised by the answer. The older man continued, "God has been very good to our family, and, as the father of this family, I have to give him thanks. When our family needs us, we have to be available. When our country needs us, we have to be willing. When God blesses us, we have to give thanks." As the young man recounted the story, he held out three fingers and touched each one of them as he recounted his grandfather's list. I could tell that the young man had taken the list to heart and let the items therein become ingrained in his own mind and heart.

What the older man was describing was virtue and—in terms of God—the virtue of religion. Nowadays, virtue is outside the context of many younger people's minds and worldviews. But virtue is an inner strength, for men and women. It is something we are called to as human beings. This grandfather knew virtue, he lived it, and he enjoyed its rewards. Do we?

Do we understand our interior call to a life of virtue? In particular, do we realize our summons to the virtue of religion?

Virtue and its reward

God calls us to do good works. When we intentionally do good works, and choose to repeat them in a consistent way, we develop a virtue. Simply put, a virtue is a good habit. Virtues become a type of second nature to us. We grow and become more ourselves through virtue.

Virtue is best understood, therefore, as a good habit that governs human action and orders its passions, combats the consequences of our fallenness, guides our conduct according to faith and reason, and helps us to restore our identity (lost by sin) in the grace of God.

Virtue accomplishes these tasks by giving us the power to do good and avoid evil. It empowers us to make the right choice, at the right time, in the right situation. It is the guardian of our freedom. Virtue is the practical means by which grace ennobles our freedom to fulfill the call of the Lord Jesus:

> You shall love the Lord your God with all your heart, and with all your soul, and with all your mind. This is the great and first commandment. And a second is like it, You shall love your neighbor as yourself (Matt. 22:37–39).

It is for this reason that St. Paul praises our freedom and connects it to the presence of the Holy Spirit. He writes:

> For freedom Christ has set us free; stand fast therefore, and do not submit again to a yoke of slavery (Gal. 5:1).

And again, the apostle writes:

> Now the Lord is the Spirit, and where the Spirit of the Lord is, there is freedom (2 Cor. 3:17).

And so, as the moral law secures freedom, so the law and freedom become the means for grace to ennoble a person to exercise virtue. Examples of virtues include the theological (or supernatural) virtues of faith, hope, and love, as well as the cardinal virtues of prudence, justice, temperance, and fortitude. Other virtues include patience, compassion, gentleness, self-control, and generosity.

For the Christian believer, virtue is the Lord's daily call, which instructs him on what to do in his life. There is nothing more tangible and practical in this world than virtue and the grace expressed through it. Virtue is more real than the physical objects of the world. It shows the world holiness. It helps the human family to see, hear, taste, smell, and touch God's presence among us.

St. John gives expression to the tangibility of grace in our lives when he writes:

[We declare to you that which] was from the beginning, which we have heard, which we have seen with our eyes, which we have looked upon and touched with our hands, concerning the word of life—the life was made manifest, and we saw it, and testify to it, and proclaim to you the eternal life which was with the Father and was made manifest to us—that which we have seen and heard we proclaim also to you, so that you may have fellowship with us; and our fellowship is with the Father and with his Son Jesus Christ. And we are writing this that our joy may be complete (1 John 1:1–4).

Since our nature is fallen, virtues can be difficult to form. Our sinfulness takes away from who we are and actually makes us less ourselves.

As a human family, we can see our sinfulness: from egregious examples like concentration camps and killing fields, to racism and violent religious extremism, to our daily battles with lust, pride, and greed. Such evils eat away at our ontological selves—that is, our existential and spiritual selves.

For this reason, the Church understands evil as a privation of being. God created all things good:

And God saw everything that he had made, and behold, it was very good (Gen. 1:31).

In seeing that the world and the human person are good and have a natural orientation to goodness (although heavily influenced by an impulse to evil), it becomes clear that sin is a privation—a lacking or removal of being, something that takes away from who I am and from my inherent goodness as a human being.

In seeing evil as a privation, we understand that sin is not a natural portion of creation and of humanity. It is not truly human or real. It is actually anti-human and anti-reality. It is like a cancer that gnaws away at the core and fabric of who we are. Sin eats away the richness of our human essence and veils our goodness as the children of God.

We are called, therefore, to fight sin and to allow grace to work in our lives. Grace seeks to bring about virtue, that type of "second nature" within us, but we have to cooperate with grace and seek virtue in our lives. In this way, virtue helps us to become more ourselves.

As the exemplar of humanity, Jesus Christ is without sin, so he is the perfect teacher in showing us how to live as full human beings. These truths are expressed throughout the New Testament.

May the God of steadfastness and encouragement grant you to live in such harmony with one another, in accord with Christ Jesus (Rom. 15:5).

For our sake he made him to be sin who knew no sin, so that in him we might become the righteousness of God (2 Cor. 5:21).

Have this mind among yourselves, which was in Christ Jesus (Phil. 2:5).

For we have not a high priest who is unable to sympathize with our weaknesses, but one who in every respect has been tempted as we are, yet without sinning (Heb. 4:15).

You know that he appeared to take away sins, and in him there is no sin (1 John 3:5).

As the savior of humanity, and the source of reconciliation between God and man, Jesus Christ takes away our sins and allows us to be free to live out our inheritance as children of God. Humanity, therefore, is defined by goodness and love.

As Pope St. John Paul II taught: "We are not the sum of our weaknesses and failures. We are the sum of the Father's love for us and our real capacity to become the image of his Son."

We were made in the image and likeness of God, and so we were created to be like him. Our entire existence is designed, hardwired, and interiorly composed to reflect his goodness and holiness. When we exercise virtue, we manifest grace—God's presence and life—in our souls and in the particular state of affairs around us.

Virtue, therefore, is a working of grace. It is a push for holiness within us. It's an interior summons to be like God. Although virtue is not easy in our fallen condition, when it triumphs, it gives us existential joy and a spirit of peace. God is with us. When we develop virtue, we are more ourselves, more who God has created us to be. This is summarized in the spiritual maxim: "Become who you are."

St. Paul expressed the victory of grace and virtue when he wrote:

> For I through the law died to the law, that I might live to God. I have been crucified with Christ; it is no longer I who live, but Christ who lives in me; and the life I now live in the flesh I live by faith in the Son of God, who loved me and gave himself for me (Gal. 2:19–20).

An example might help us to consolidate our presentation of sin as diminishing our moral goodness, the workings of grace within us, and the development of virtue as a means to becoming more ourselves in Jesus Christ.

Years ago, I worked with an amazing Catholic outreach program that assists men and women who suffer from alcohol, drug, and porn addictions. The community follows the simple principle of *ora et labora*—pray and work. The recovering addicts work throughout the day in hard manual labor. The work pauses only for prayer and meals. As the prayer is interspersed throughout the day, it becomes the real heart of the person's day and his overall recovery.

Sometimes talking is allowed during the day's work session. Conversations have to be uplifting and encouraging. On one such occasion, I was walking with a young man who shared his story with me.

He had been an honor student, accomplished in sports, and well liked by everyone. As a consequence of his social life, he flirted with marijuana. Over time, peer pressure led him to pursue harder drugs. Unlike the previous flirting, these drugs took hold of him. He described how they took over his life. The drugs became the focus of everything. They took away his intellect, his work ethic, his talents, his sense of humor, his friends, and eventually his family. He explained how on one occasion, he physically assaulted his mother because he wanted money to buy drugs.

The young man said he felt like a stranger to himself. He would hear himself say things and not believe he was saying them. He did things that scandalized and shocked himself. He often thought, "Who is this? What's happening to me?" But these moments of awareness would soon pass as the thirst for drugs would overtake him, and the cycle would continue.

Eventually, he was forced to get help. He tried to fight it, but he failed. He had no appeal. As he entered the community, his withdrawal from drugs was excruciating. His body shook uncontrollably, and he felt completely lost.

The withdrawal passed, and he began the long path of recovery. In the course of time, he regained more of his mental capacity. He was assigned cooking duties and attempted some creative food options. He picked up the guitar and let another community member teach him how to play. As he told me, "I was getting my life back." And as a biblical encouragement, he took the words spoken by the father about his prodigal son in the famous parable:

> For this my son was dead, and is alive again; he was lost, and is found (Luke 15:24).

In this account, we see the cancerous effects of sin on the soul, as the young man became a stranger to himself. We also see the restorative power of grace and the life-giving effects of virtue as he was getting his life back. In this way, sin takes away from who we are, whereas grace and virtue help us become more ourselves.

As human beings, we are naturally oriented to virtue. When we decline this call, we become less ourselves. If such negligence is perpetuated, then we become strangers even to our own selves. Virtue is a spiritual freedom, an awareness of our true selves, and a powerful source of grace in our lives.

The call to virtue includes worship. Despite modern efforts to dismiss worship or to turn it into some form of entertainment or self-worship, there is a clear call (and need) for authentic worship in every human heart. This need is fulfilled by the faithful exercise of the virtue of religion.

The virtue of religion

As human beings, we have been made by and for God. As such, we have also been created for worship. We have a fundamental, existential need to offer true worship to the living God. He is our everything, and if this is not acknowledged and its exercise does not become the center of our lives, then we drift aimlessly from one form of emotional fulfillment to another. We will have fragmented lives, with no lasting foundation and no source of enduring joy.

Our life truly begins and finds its deepest meaning in the worship of God. It is an unavoidable decision: will we humble ourselves and worship the living God? Or will we deny this call to worship, or manipulate it into some form of self-worship?

In the broadest terms possible, God is our eternal Creator, who cares for us by his divine Providence. As such, we owe him our homage and gratitude. This debt of sorts falls under the virtue of justice. Justice is to give someone his due. God is due our reverence and esteem. Under the umbrella of justice, therefore, we recognize the specific virtue of religion.

Located within the realm of the virtue of justice, religion ranks supreme among other virtues, since it involves our relationship with God.

The virtue of religion is the command within our souls to acknowledge God's goodness to us, humble ourselves, and give him proper honor and adoration. This reverence includes the duty of worship. If someone wants to live a full life, existentially satisfied with peace in his heart, then he must exercise the virtue of religion and properly worship God.

The word *religion* comes from a Latin word meaning "to bind oneself." Properly understood, it is the perfect word for this pre-eminent virtue, since religion is a binding of ourselves to God, a proper worship of him, a way of life and a community that flows from that worship, as well as the many customs and traditions that surround such a community and way of life.

The virtue of religion is a binding. It is a recognition that our lives are not only about ourselves. Religion includes a death to self, the joining of a community, and a commitment to true worship. The virtue of religion begins with a free choice by each of us to reciprocate God's love, to give him his due, and to properly worship him above all things. This is the virtue of religion. This is what each person is called to accept and to integrate into his own life. Have we?

Knowing our fallenness, and desiring to provide his divine assistance, God included in his revelation the path and instructions for true worship. Since our worship of him is so united to our existential well-being, God provided us with the all the means of authentically and fully worshipping him with true mind and sincere heart.

Are we open to God's revealed worship in our lives? Are we willing to die to our narcissism and self-worship and accept his path to true worship?

The Biblical History of Worship

In his continued goodness to us, God has not only revealed the knowledge he has of himself, but also revealed to the human family how we are to worship him. In our fallenness, we are inclined to self-worship, to manipulate even the homage due to God, and to settle for the contingent things offered by this world rather than the eternal and splendorous things offered by God and an authentic worship of him. Here's a story that can help illustrate this point.

When I was in graduate school, I went with some friends to North Africa. We arranged for a small van, driver, and bodyguard to take us into the Sahara to one of the ancient monasteries of the Christian faith. We wanted to see where St. Anthony of Egypt, hailed in his day as the holiest man alive, lived and prayed.

The drive took hours. The sun was scorching. We finally arrived, and one of the monks greeted us.

After an initial conversation outside, in which the monk tried to figure out who we were, since no pre-arrangements had been made, we were welcomed into the monastery. The entire experience was surreal. The monastery looked like pictures from the fourth century. It was like walking into the world of St. Anthony, which hadn't changed in almost 1,600 years. We were given a brief tour and then offered some food.

After our meal, when the monk realized our faith, we were taken on a second tour, which I later called the "real tour." In this second tour, we saw areas of the cloistered part of the monastery and shown some of the vessels used for worship. Then—the best part—we were taken to a small chapel with a tightly enclosed entrance. We were told that this is where Anthony would offer the divine liturgy. It's where St. Athanasius would come and pray when he had to flee Alexandria as he defended the divinity of Jesus Christ.

The history was powerful enough, but then to walk into the small chapel was an experience all its own. The altar is shaped like the Ark of the Covenant; it even has four horns on the four sides, jutting out as we could imagine the horns of the ark did themselves. Along the walls were etched images of Old Testament sacrifices, and then, as you looked up, the curved wall, that almost touched our heads, had the most majestic, terrifying images of the Four Living Creatures that I have ever seen. They were depicted as hovering over the altar, waiting for the Word to become flesh. It was breathtaking, beautiful, powerful, and out of this world.

In thinking of that chapel and Athanasius fleeing to that monastery in times of persecution, confusion, and isolation, I realized that he went to a place of silence and revealed truth so he could pray and worship. He was seeking strength and encouragement. He didn't turn to emotionally charged music, or a motivational speaker, or flashing lights, or clapping hands, or any of the modern things we are told are "worship."

No, the great champion who defended our Lord's divinity—who was mocked with the slogan "Athanasius against the world"—didn't have time for such self-indulgence. He needed a strong soul, he needed true worship, because he needed to encounter and receive power from the living God. And so, Athanasius turned to the divine liturgy, to the worship given to us by God himself. He worshipped God on God's terms, and so he sought to die to himself that he might rise and live in Jesus Christ.

This is true worship, and the holy ones model it for us. Throughout salvation history, God has desired to guide and show us the path to worship him and bind ourselves to him. Will we listen, and will we allow ourselves to be led?

In the beginning

At the beginning of time, God created all things good. He crowned his creation with Adam and Eve. He loved them and gave them a share in his own life. As a part of this divine life, they were given freedom. This freedom was bestowed so that they might reciprocate his love. And such love would be given back by the obedience and homage of worship. Our first parents would share in God's love by worshipping him.

As God has done throughout salvation history, so he did in the Garden of Eden. He gave the means and the way to worship him—namely, love one another, bring forth life, care for the garden, and do not eat from the Tree of the Knowledge of Good and Evil (Gen. 2:15–17). True love always has options, and Adam and Eve had a choice. Worship involves choices and opportunities to surrender our lives to God.

The garden stood as a pre-temple, Adam was a proto-priest, and the positive and negative commands of the garden were worship instructions. In such a state, the angels marveled and wondered: will the children of God worship?

Adam and Eve chose not to worship—or, at least, not to worship God. Our first parents listened to whispered lies and deceptions (Gen. 3:1–7). They indulged their own hearts and fell into a subjective, relativistic worldview that led them to disobey their loving Father and to praise and worship themselves. And so, the human family, and the creation under its care, fell from grace. We chose ourselves over God, self-worship over the life-giving worship of the true and living God.

This fall from grace is the source of all chaos and every sin in our world today. It seeks to repeat itself, to procreate its rebellion, and this particularly happens in idolatry, in false worship, and most egregiously in self-worship. When we turn to our own emotional fulfillment, our own euphoria, our own self-affirmation and self-actualization, then we leave the world of true worship and of the authentic virtue of religion.

We continue to see this twist and turn throughout the story of salvation.

Worship and salvation history

From the fall and our expulsion from the Garden of Eden, throughout salvation history, we see constant examples of our call to truly worship God with our whole hearts.

After our first parents, we see their sons, Cain and Abel, called to worship. Cain is a farmer and offers the Lord God a sacrifice from the earth (Gen. 4:2, 4). Abel is a shepherd and does likewise. Cain's offering, however, is refused (v. 5). This leads Cain into anger. We see a pattern: false worship leads to rejection, which then leads to darkness and great sin. Cain takes his brother's life, the first time human blood touches the earth (v. 8).

What happened with Cain's offering? We are told in the sacred narrative that Abel offered "fat portions" (which was considered the choicest part of the animal) and the "first-lings"—the best—of his flock (Gen. 4:4). Meanwhile, Cain offered only a general and empty offering of "the fruit of the ground" (v. 3). His offering gave nothing of the heart; it involved no real sacrifice at all in terms of his crops and harvest. He gave a meager offering, reflecting a distracted and covetous soul. It was false worship because it was self-regarding worship.

The Genesis account provides a helpful description. Later in the New Testament, however, the letter to the Hebrews gives us a fuller explanation:

> By faith Abel offered to God a more acceptable sacrifice than Cain, through which he received approval as

righteous, God bearing witness by accepting his gifts; he died, but through his faith he is still speaking (11:4).

In the biblical accounts, we can see that Abel offered a higher gift, the best from his flock, and it was also his faith that made his offering acceptable. This is an important point. In true worship, we must offer God our best, and we must have faith in him as the offering is made. We don't offer God mere entertainment, or the whimsical expression of our emotions; we are called to do the real work of worship and to offer God our whole selves, and to have faith in him as the sacrifice is made (see Rom. 12:1–2).

As we leave Cain and Abel and walk through salvation history, we come to Abraham and Melchizedek. After winning a great victory over several towns, Abram (the future Abraham) accepts the blessing of the "priest of God Most High" and joins in his worship, marked by the offering of bread and wine, by granting a tenth of his bounty to the offering (Gen. 14:18–20). In a few small verses, we see a glimpse of the early worship of God's people. Here, the mysterious figure of Melchizedek, later emphasized in the New Testament in the letter to the Hebrews, leads the great patriarch in worship. And Abram lets himself be directed in worship. He's not worried about personal fulfillment, or emotional satisfaction, or mere human culture. Abram is heartfelt and committed to worship, even offering a tenth of his bounty in the sacrifice.

After the time of Abraham and the great patriarchs of old, we witness the enslavement of Israel in Egypt. After the

Israelites endure four hundred years in slavery, God raises up Moses and comes to ransom his people. God calls his people to worship, but Pharaoh will not let them go (Exod. 3:1–12; 5:1–4). God unleashes ten plagues upon the land. Each of the ten plagues parallels a false god of Egypt and humbles the polytheistic Egyptians in their misplaced worship (Exod. 7–12). Only after the night of Passover, which becomes memorialized as an annual liturgical act of worship among the chosen people, does Pharaoh let Israel go.

Once on the path to freedom, it becomes clear that Israel has been taken out of Egypt, but Egypt has not been taken out of Israel. The chosen people are still tied to the worship and false security of their former captives. And so, for the first time in salvation history, God institutes formal animal sacrifice. He takes the priesthood from the families of Israel and reserves it to the tribe of Levi as a reward for its fidelity in refusing to worship the Golden Calf with the other tribes of Israel (Exod. 32:25–29). The chosen people were called out of Egypt for worship, but it's clear that such worship requires discipline. God, therefore, is teaching and dictating how his children are to worship him. God does not take worship lightly. He knows the hearts of his people. He is not concerned with how they feel, or about Israel's respectability among the other nations. He is attentive to his people and their right worship of him.

The truth is clear: if you get worship right, you'll get life right. If you get worship wrong, you'll get life wrong. Everything rises or falls with worship.

In the course of time, Israel as a confederation of tribes gives way to Israel as a national monarchy. The first king, Saul, loses both his dynasty and his own crown because of false or incomplete worship (1 Sam. 13:5–14; 15:13–31). Israel's second king, David, God's chosen one (16:1), is named and first anointed during worship (vv. 1–13). He is "a man after [God's] own heart" (13:14) and places worship at the center of his life and of his reign over Israel. As David's throne is blessed in perpetuity, so a new priesthood foreshadowed and prepared for. It will not be a priesthood of the Levites, nor of hereditary duties, but a priesthood that harkens back to a time of earlier innocence. It will be a priesthood in the Order of Melchizedek, with a "thanksgiving sacrifice" of bread and wine. Melchizedek first offered such a sacrifice in the time of Abraham (Gen. 14:18-20). It will become the sacrifice of the Messiah—with bread becoming flesh and wine becoming blood—the one sacrifice that will endure when all other sacrifices are ended.

Foreshadowing this priesthood, David exercises priestly functions, which was uncommon for non-Levites at the time, when he brings the Ark of the Covenant to Jerusalem. David wears priestly vestment and offers sacrifice (2 Sam. 6:12–14, 17–19). Although David did not regularly function in this way, his actions did prophesy something else to come. Similar actions deprived Saul of his royal dynasty (1 Sam. 13: 5–13). For David, however, they were acceptable. They foretold a new priesthood, not yet realized, and pointed to something greater to come from the throne of David (13:14; cf. Psalm 2; Luke 20:41–44).

The tabernacle of the desert eventually became concretized in the Jerusalem temple. After King Solomon, David's successor, builds the temple, God orders all worship of God on the cliffs and in the high places to be stopped (see Deut. 12:1–14, 2 Kings 18:4, 2 Kings 23:8, John 4:20). For Jewish worship had become loose, taking on cultural elements outside the commands of God. Idolatry, the perpetual threat to true worship of the living God, was seeping into the ceremonies of the various cities. Beyond politics, worship was to be centralized in Jerusalem and done solely in the temple there. In this action, God was once again calling his people to authentic worship. He was streamlining the worship of Israel in order to free it from idolatrous influences and to lead his people to true and life-giving worship.

Eventually, even the temple itself became contaminated by greed, duplicity, and false worship. In response, there was an immense backlash by the prophets. The prophetic chastisement of the temple and of insincere or sacrilegious worship was severe. God's people were once again replacing worship with something else. They sought their own comfort, power, emotional fulfillment, and political gain. The chosen people did not want to accept the demands of authentic worship, and, in their negligence, they rebelled against the living God. The prophetic denunciations went unheeded, and so God allowed his people to be divided and for his own temple to be demolished. The destruction of the temple was devastating, one of the most traumatizing events in salvation history.

After the exile of God's people to Babylonia, they returned and built the second temple (2 Chron. 36:22–23; Ezra 1:1–4). The Ark of the Covenant was never found and remains lost to this day. The second temple never held the glorious inheritance of Solomon's temple:

> Speak now to Zerub'babel the son of She-al'ti-el, governor of Judah, and to Joshua the son of Jeho'zadak, the high priest, and to all the remnant of the people, and say, "Who is left among you that saw this house in its former glory? How do you see it now? Is it not in your sight as nothing? Yet now take courage, O Zerub'babel, says the Lord; take courage, O Joshua, son of Jeho'zadak, the high priest; take courage, all you people of the land, says the Lord; work, for I am with you, says the Lord of hosts, according to the promise that I made you when you came out of Egypt. My Spirit abides among you; fear not" (Hag. 2:2–5).

With the loss of the ark, worship had to be adjusted, and such revisions were annual reminders to God's people of what was lost and why it was allowed to be taken. As the Greeks moved in and occupied the promised land, they desecrated the second temple, and many of the chosen people allowed it and became accomplices to its defilement (2 Macc. 6:1–12). Authentic worship was replaced by idolatry, and vanity and a desire for respectability among unbelievers were the rule of the day. Enculturation became a cover for apostasy and syncretism. In response, the noble Maccabee family revolted and sought to bring Israel back to an obedience of God's law and to restore the temple's integrity of worship (ch. 8).

The Greeks gave way to the Romans, who constantly pushed against the faith of Israel and sought its absorption into Rome's morphed universalized pantheon of many gods from many different lands.

During the famed *Pax Romana*, when the world was at peace under the governance of Caesar Augustus, the "fullness of time" came upon us, and the long-awaited Messiah was "born of woman, born under the law" (Gal. 4:4–5). The promise of a savior given at Eden (Gen. 3:15), which was prepared for and stretched through the ages from Noah, Abraham, Moses, and David, now found its fulfillment. As announced by the angel: "He will be great, and will be called the Son of the Most High; and the Lord God will give to him the throne of his father David" (Luke 1:32).

The Son of David, the "Wonderful Counselor, Mighty God, Everlasting Father, Prince of Peace" (Isa. 9:6), came to redeem the human family. This redemption would take the form of an acceptable sacrifice that would be the fulfillment of the Passover, the definitive Bread of the Presence, and the everlasting thanksgiving offering (*todah* in Hebrew, *eucharistia* in Greek).

The long-awaited Messiah, Jesus Christ, the God-Man, offered this sacrifice in his paschal mystery—namely, in his passion, death, and resurrection. It is a mystery that is re-presented by the power of the Holy Spirit wherever the breaking of the bread—the *todah*, the *eucharistia*—is celebrated. This is the fulfillment of all sacrifices.

As the letter to the Hebrews teaches: "[Christ] entered once for all into the Holy Place, taking not the blood of goats and calves but his own blood, thus securing an eternal redemption" (9:12), and: "But when Christ had offered for all time a single sacrifice for sins, he sat down at the right hand of God. . . . For by a single offering he has perfected for all time those who are sanctified" (10:12, 14).

Spirit and truth

The Lord Jesus prepared his disciples for this sacrifice on Calvary. In his public ministry, he summarized the whole of salvation history in his discourse with the Samaritan woman at Jacob's Well. It is the longest recorded one-on-one conversation between the Lord and another person. In the exchange, the woman—a symbol of the rebellious Northern Kingdom—seeks to shame or silence the Lord, but the Lord is calling Samaria back to God's covenant. As such, it is no surprise that the discourse begins to revolve around worship.

As Jesus initiates the conversation, the woman protests, "How is it that you, a Jew, ask a drink of me, a woman of Samar'ia?" (John 4:9). The Lord tells the woman that if she knew who he was, *she* would be asking *him* for something to drink. In response, the woman questions his ability to provide water: "the woman said to him, 'Sir, you have no bucket, and the well is deep; where do you get that living water?'" (v. 11, NRSVCE). As the discourse continues, the woman says to him, "Sir, I perceive that you are a prophet. Our fathers worshipped on this mountain; and you say that in Jerusalem is the place where men ought to worship" (vv. 19–20).

Jesus replies,

Woman, believe me, the hour is coming when neither on this mountain nor in Jerusalem will you worship the Father. You worship what you do not know; we worship what we know, for salvation is from the Jews. But the hour is coming, and now is, when the true worshippers will worship the Father in spirit and truth, for such the Father seeks to worship him. God is spirit, and those who worship him must worship in spirit and truth (vv. 21–24).

As the Lord fulfills the messianic mission of reuniting the tribes of Israel, he readies to bring the Northern Kingdom back into the covenant, and to extend the blessings of Israel upon all the nations. The Lord Jesus indicates that "the temple" will no longer be in Jerusalem and that all of God's children will worship him "in spirit and truth." The Lord is bringing prophecy to completion and readying the hearts of the chosen people for the final and definitive temple of his body, and the everlasting Passover sacrifice of his broken body and outpoured blood, under the appearance of the bread and wine of the *todah*, the *eucharistia*, the eternal thanksgiving offering of the Messiah.

The eternal temple

The second temple never held the glory of Solomon's temple. The loss of the Ark of the Covenant was a perpetual reminder of the fall of the first temple. The building of the second temple was thought to initiate the time of the New Jerusalem and the age of the Messiah, but such hopes were quickly proven wrong.

At the time of the Lord Jesus, the second temple had recently undergone an almost five-decade renovation. As such, the temple was the pride of the chosen people, especially as they were under an occupation by the Gentile Roman power. The temple became more a source of political power and of greed than a source of religion and worship. In such a state, the second temple proved that it was ill conceived and devoid of God's presence.

In fulfilling the prophetic denunciations of the temple, therefore, the Lord Jesus purified the second temple of its sacrilege (John 2:13–17). Such action was not only punitive. It was also a declaration of a new and everlasting worship of the living God.

When asked by what authority he purified the temple, the Lord responds:

"Destroy this temple, and in three days I will raise it up." The Jews then said, "It has taken forty-six years to build this temple, and will you raise it up in three days?" But he spoke of the temple of his body. When therefore he was raised from the dead, his disciples remembered that he had said this; and they believed the scripture and the word which Jesus had spoken (John 2:19–22).

At face value, the Lord's answer is offensive to the priestly class, who are Sadducees and do not believe in the resurrection of the dead. Beyond that, the answer indicates a future reality. The Lord Jesus is giving us a glimpse into the worship of God "in spirit and truth."

In responding to the challenge, the Lord apparently tells his listeners to tear down the second temple. They respond with a historical answer. But we're then told that the Lord is speaking of "the temple of his body." The temple was supposed to be the place of God's presence. The second temple was found lacking, but the Lord Jesus is pointing us to his body as a new temple, a new place of his presence, a new nexus for worship, and the source of a new priesthood. The Lord Jesus is preparing his apostles and disciples for the paschal mystery and for the institution of the eucharistic sacrifice, which will be the eternal worship of God in spirit and in truth by all men (John 4:23–24; see also Rev. 5:6–14; 13:8).

This same preparation and prophetic instruction is given by the Lord Jesus in his bread of life discourse (John 6:22–59). The Lord boldly proclaims: "I am the bread of life; he who comes to me shall not hunger, and he who believes in me shall never thirst" (v. 35).

After the Lord's passion, death, and resurrection, the worship of God is elevated. Worship is perfected in the breaking of the bread, where the one, historical eucharistic sacrifice of the Lord Jesus, God-Man and Messiah, is re-presented by the power of the Holy Spirit to his followers throughout the ages. In this sacrifice, the source and summit of the entire Christian way of life, the virtue of religion is perfectly fulfilled, and the worship of the living God can find no greater expression.

In his mystical visions, while seeing heavenly realities and the glory of the Lord's sacrifice in paradise, John hears a voice crying out: "Behold, the dwelling of God is with men. He will dwell with them, and they shall be his people, and God himself will be with them" (Rev. 21:3).

This is the fruition of the Lord Jesus' words to the Samaritan woman. It is the Lord providing us with the true worship of God, the worship "in spirit and truth."

As Christians, do we understand what has been given to us? Do we realize the infinite sacredness of the eucharistic sacrifice? Do we seek to approach and worship God with clean, attentive, and loving hearts?

Biblical Marks of Worship

Recently, a university chaplain shared me with the homily he gives on the first Sunday of every new semester. Realizing that many of the students might find themselves in various forms of grave sin, and that often such guilt from those sins makes the students disappear from religious worship, the chaplain describes the Mass and explains that life will be good and bad, ugly and beautiful, and we'll do things—both good and evil—that we never imagined. As life has its ups and downs, the one stable thing is the Lord Jesus and the sacrificial love he has for each of us. As the Carthusian order reminds us all, "while the world spins, the cross stands firm."

The chaplain then explains that the holy sacrifice of the Mass is the most immediate and sure way in which we participate in, and receive, the sacrificial love of the Lord Jesus. After making these points, the chaplain gives an exhortation and plea: "And so, no matter where you find yourself, be sure that you always make it to this altar for Sunday Mass. No matter what guilt or regret is in your heart, be sure to come here. Whether you can receive Holy Communion or not, come to this altar and know how much the Lord loves you. Because if you stop coming here, you'll fade away, the Mass will no longer be a part of your life, and you'll convince yourself that you alone have to fix everything that's wrong in your life and in the world. That will crush you and make you miserable. The Lord wants you to be free and happy. And so, be sure to come to Mass—no matter what!"

The chaplain knows that the stakes are high with young believers and that worship is the making or breaking of their souls. He knows he needs them in the pews and at the holy sacrifice. Once there, grace can heal and fix whatever's happened in their souls, by the Mass and by confession. But for any of this to happen, they have to be there.

Worship is about the praise of God. It's about consistency and the forming of a habit. A good habit is virtue (and a bad habit is vice). The worship of God develops the virtue of religion in the hearts of all men and women, young and old. Gleaning from Sacred Scripture and the Christian tradition, we can identify five marks of this essential virtue.

Before listing the biblical marks of the virtue of religion, what would you cite as the identifiers of religion? In your own heart and from your own experience, what five points would you give?

Five marks of the virtue of religion

From the vast treasury of Sacred Scripture, the outline of which was given earlier in this chapter, and from Sacred Tradition, we can recognize and list five marks of the virtue of religion. Simply put:

1. Religion is the natural virtue that acknowledges God as God, who is worthy to be worshipped and obeyed.

2. Religion is the humble recognition that we are bound to God.

3. Religion is the acknowledgment of our debt to God, which cannot be repaid but must be constantly honored by true acts of homage.

4. Religion compels us to gratitude and convicts us to obey God's moral law and to follow him in our daily lives.

5. Religion shows us our connection and obligation to all other believers, both living and dead.

As a help in our future chapters, we will summarize them as follows: 1) *God as God*, 2) *Humble Recognition*, 3) *Debt to God*, 4) *Gratitude and Obedience*, and 5) *Connection to Others*.

The five marks as a template

In looking at these points from the sources of God's revelation, it's worth asking: how did my list compare? How did it contrast? This can be a helpful lesson and examination of conscience. The five marks are given here to help us understand what this virtue is calling out from us. They can guide and correct our understanding and exercise of this foundational virtue.

The five marks given in this chapter will be used as a template as we walk through the various moves and efforts to redefine the virtue of religion and to eclipse true worship with something of inferior value.

As we prepare to walk through these diverse forms of idolatry, it would be a noble practice to ready our souls by reflecting upon these five marks.

Threats to the Virtue of Religion

In this chapter, we reviewed our understanding of God, the virtue of religion, our duties and responsibilities before God, and the biblical history and marks of true religion. Regrettably, there are many threats to the authentic virtue of religion.

The first threat begins in our own souls. The Lord Jesus taught about this in his parable of the wedding banquet (Matt. 22:1–14).

In the parable, the Lord describes a king who gives a wedding banquet for his son. He sends his servants out to extend the invitation to the celebration. But those who are invited won't come. He sends his servants out again, instructing them: "Tell those who are invited, Behold, I have made ready my dinner, my oxen and my fat calves are killed, and everything is ready; come to the marriage feast" (v. 4).

Those invited again dismiss things, one going to his farm and another to his business. Some of the invitees even seize the king's servants, mistreat them, and kill them. In response, the king sends his troops, kills the murderers, and burns down their city.

Then the king says to his slaves, "The wedding is ready, but those invited were not worthy. Go therefore to the thoroughfares, and invite to the marriage feast as many as you find" (vv. 8–9).

The king's servants go out and gather everyone they find, both good and bad. As a result, the wedding hall is filled with guests.

When the king comes in to see the guests, he notices a man there who is not wearing a wedding robe. He says to him, "Friend, how did you get in here without a wedding garment?" (v. 12). The man is speechless.

Then the king says to his servants, "Bind him hand and foot, and cast him into the outer darkness; there men will weep and gnash their teeth" (v. 13).

The Lord Jesus concludes the parable by teaching, "For many are called, but few are chosen" (v. 14).

At first read, we might be caught off guard by the reaction of the king. The frustrated monarch had the people brought in from the streets. How could he attack and denounce a person for not being properly dressed?

Well, the cultural context helps us. At that time, it was a common sign of hospitality that the host would provide an outer robe to the guests, especially those who were traveling great distances. So the ill clad person in the parable is someone who chose not to accept what was offered and to dismiss the proper vestment for so great a celebration. The guest thought that just because he was invited, and chose to come, anything was acceptable. He failed to respect that he was attending a banquet in the presence of a king, and there were standards and expectations.

The cultural context of the robe is emphasized by St. Matthew, since it would have resonated with the early Christian community. In particular, the festive robe would have been clearly understood as a symbol of the baptismal garment. The Gentile Christians understood the privilege of being the "second round" of invitees to the banquet—second to the Jewish people—and would have clung to their baptismal dignity, reflected by the white garment, as a sign that they belonged in the kingdom of God (Rev. 19:8).

Drawing from the symbolism of the baptismal garment, we can broaden the meaning of the garment itself and see it as signifying a general and proper disposition of a soul ready to worship God according to his revelation and in harmony with the dictates of his covenant.

Through the lessons of this parable, therefore, we are assisted in recognizing some of the possible internal impediments to true worship. Are we willing to wear the garment that has been given to us? Or do we desire to do "our own thing" and present ourselves however we prefer? Are we ready to worship God in spirit and truth, according to his designs and his instructions? Or will we settle for the merely subjectively satisfying?

Parable of the sower

As we see an authentic worship of God and a robust exercise of the virtue of religion before us, we also have counterfeits and false goods that present themselves as equal and viable options. True religion in each of our hearts is threatened by the allure of sentiment, the results of self-help, the choice of commodity, the easiness of mere culture, and the power of politics. Each of these presents itself as an option, when all of them are really only idols dressed up and made to look sophisticated and satisfying. But they are lies, and they lead us away from God and the exercise of authentic religion.

Another parable can help us. On one occasion during the Lord Jesus' public ministry, he left the house where he was staying and sat beside the sea. The crowds saw him and gathered around him. The people became so numerous that he had to sit on a boat so as to be seen and to preach to the large group. In his preaching, he told them the parable of the sower (Matt. 13:1–9).

The parable is known to many of us. It's worth repeating, and it can guide us in understanding the attack on true worship and religion in our world today.

The Lord Jesus says to us,

A sower went out to sow. And as he sowed, some seeds fell along the path, and the birds came and devoured them. Other seeds fell on rocky ground, where they had not much soil, and immediately they sprang up, since they had no depth of soil, but when the sun rose they were scorched; and since they had no root they withered away. Other seeds fell upon thorns, and the thorns grew up and choked them. Other seeds fell on good soil and brought forth grain, some a hundredfold, some sixty, some thirty. He who has ears, let him hear (Matt. 13:3-9).

And so, the seeds are threatened by the birds, the heat of the sun, and the thorns. True worship and the virtue of religion are threatened by external entities as well. Not only must we guard our hearts, but we must watch the things that influence us and shape our souls. True religion must be watchful of the symbolic birds of sentiment and self-help, the burning sun of commodity, and the thorns of social activism. Each of these, although perhaps good in itself, becomes disastrous when it overtakes and eclipses worship and religion.

Have we fallen prey to these threats? Can we discern and identify their dark influence on our souls and recognize how they affect our worship? Are we willing to openly identify these threats and seek to worship God in spirit and in truth?

The task ahead

These four threats will be researched in the remaining four chapters of this book. We will explore the misplacement of sentiment, self-help, commodity, mere culture, and politics in worship and religion.

God is calling each of us, his children, to know him, love him, worship him, and serve him. He calls out to us as our loving Father who seeks our companionship. He sent his Son, our Lord, to show us the way to his love. He has revealed his heart to us so that we can worship him without fear, holy and righteous in his sight, all the days of our lives (see Luke 1:74–75).

Our exposition, therefore, is done so that we can see the freedom and joy of right worship and true religion. Our task is not simply to unmask idols, but to build up our understanding of worship and our comprehension of religion.

The first threat to true religion is *sentiment*. And so, let's begin!

2

WHEN RELIGION BECOMES SENTIMENT

My soul longs, yea, faints
for the courts of the Lord;
my heart and my flesh sing for joy
to the living God.

—Psalm 84:2

Throughout my priestly ministry, I have always heavily preached the importance of frequent confession. In my homiletics, I stress the spiritual goods of the sacrament and their effects on our souls. Regrettably, many of the faithful dismiss the invitation and settle for the oftentimes tragic minimum of once a year. Every once in a while, however, someone will be stirred by the Holy Spirit and will start going to regular confession.

On one such occasion, a middle-aged woman (not from my current parish assignment) accepted the call and started going to confession monthly. After a few months, she asked to see me and discuss her reception of the sacrament. I was overjoyed and expected a serious conversation on aspects of ascetical theology. I was wrong. The conversation started amicably enough, but then it quickly spiraled downward. The woman expressed frustration not only with the sacrament, but with me. She indicated that she had accepted the call to make regular confessions, changed her schedule to accommodate her new resolution, and then dove into various resources to prepare well for the sacrament. Everything seemed fine in her explanation, so I was curious to see what was causing the frustration. I didn't have to wait long.

After giving a summary of her noble efforts, she told me, "Father, I did all those things, and I've received confession every month, and you know what? I didn't feel anything. It made no difference. What's the point?"

I was surprised. Did this Christian believer hear what she had just said? Did she realize what she had just said? Did she really mean it?

After a pause, I noted, "But it sounds like you've made good confessions." The woman nodded, and so I continued, "Well, then, your sins are forgiven, and God's grace has been poured into your heart. What else were you expecting?"

The woman looked at me as I must have been looking at her, and she responded, "Comfort! Or something. I hear all these stories about people coming out of the confessional and feeling lighter and better and more motivated. I thought I'd feel *something*."

Okay, now I understood, and so I asked her, "Do you know that your sins were forgiven, and that grace was given to you, even though you didn't feel it?" Her response was as shocking as it was scandalous. She said in a matter-of-fact tone, "But if I don't feel it, what's the point?"

I couldn't believe my ears. Did this Christian really just make those comments? I waited and then followed up.

"Well, the point is that your sins were *really* removed, you were *really* given grace, and however your emotions did (or did not) respond has nothing to do with *the reality*. Your sins were forgiven! You have received grace, which is God's own life and power. This is reality!"

The conversation didn't get any better. To my knowledge, the woman stopped going to confession because she didn't feel consoled and decided that God had somehow failed her and had not fulfilled his part of her presumed bargain.

The conversation was difficult, to say the least. It's hard even to relay now in this book. And yet, we see the widespread belief in the West, even among Christian believers, that religion and worship should spark our emotions and make us feel good. The wayward conclusion is reached: if they cannot accomplish the demands of sentiment, then they aren't worth doing. This is the sad, false reality that occurs when religion becomes sentiment.

This state of affairs raises some questions. How are we supposed to understand the proper place of sentiment in religion and worship? Is sentiment always a bad thing? Can the virtue of religion withstand a coup d'état by sentiment?

The Heart

In our desire to accept the path of true worship, there are some struggles along the way. We are fallen, and in our fallenness, we are inclined to incomplete worship or even to a well disguised self-worship. In particular, our sentiments and emotions want to corrode reality and make our hearts the center of all things. With that temptation before us, we have to clarify what our heart is, why we've been created with sentiments and emotions, and how we are to understand them.

As human beings, made in the image of God, we have a self-possession born from our spiritual souls. This self-possession is the ground upon which we share in God's own divine reason. It is the basis upon which our sentiments move.

Biblically, our self-possession is referred to as "the heart," which the *Catechism of the Catholic Church* calls our hidden center, the place of truth, decision, covenant, and the arena where we encounter God (2563).

And so, when the Bible speaks of "the heart," it is not referring to the epicenter of our emotions, or even to how we "feel" in the popular sense, but rather to the place where truth is discovered (not invented) and where we are revealed to ourselves and where we encounter the living God.

In a moral sense, "the heart" is also a reference to our conscience. But just as the heart has been redefined in our modern world, so has the conscience. Properly understood, the conscience is the inner sanctuary of the person, where he communicates not only with himself, but also with God. There, in the hidden meeting place of his interior life, the moral law and the person's freedom interact and make decisions.

In understanding the conscience in this way, we can see it as the place of unity between the moral law and freedom. It is in the heart, a person's conscience, that the moral law tempers freedom and spares it from becoming an idol, as it reveals the moral law and commands our freedom to obey it. In a similar fashion, freedom empowers the moral law for the growth of virtue and holiness. A mature conscience, therefore, does not seek to be freed from truth, but sees truth as the means by which it can be truly free and grow in goodwill as a child of God.

If a person does not have some form of an interior life, and lacks an attentive ear to his conscience, then he can be easily misled regarding what is true, good, and beautiful.

The conscience is not some type of divine oracle sent down from the gods upon the mind of a person, nor is it merely our personal wish or some type of a superego, nor is it the consensus of a group of voices within the person. The conscience is not where we figure things out for ourselves, or where we find emotional fulfillment, or where we create our own reality. These are the exact opposite of the conscience.

The conscience, our spiritual heart, is a witness to God, truth, and goodness. It is a voice of judgment within us, which concludes what is good and what is evil. It penetrates the entirety of our souls. As such, it convicts us and frees us from relativism and a misplaced self-satisfied life.

At times, sentiment assaults our hearts, and we are tempted to compromise with evil, to betray goodness or to redefine it. Though good and oriented toward goodness, the human heart is also fallen. It can betray itself and its own mission in our interior lives. The prophet Jeremiah rightly warns us:

> The heart is deceitful above all things, and desperately corrupt; who can understand it? (Jer. 17:9).

In his public ministry, the Lord Jesus was cautious of the human heart:

> Now when he was in Jerusalem at the Passover feast, many believed in his name when they saw the signs which he did; but Jesus did not trust himself to them, because he knew all men and needed no one to bear witness of man; for he himself knew what was in man (John 2:23–25).

In moments of temptation or duplicity, treachery or sentimentality, the strength of a truly well formed conscience will clarify any confusion, convict us, and guide us to remaining faithful to virtue and its demands.

In particular, if sentiment overtakes our conscience, then we are imprisoned in a small, self-created world, where good and evil become whatever we think or feel they should be. In such a dark world, we become slaves to the whims, shallowness, and cruelty of our own emotions. In this process, our sentiments demand that we worship them. By adhering to this false worship, we end up worshipping ourselves.

Any attempted usurpation over our souls by sentiment, therefore, needs to be addressed and redirected by a strong heart—invigorated by virtue, especially the virtue of religion and its call to worship God and God alone.

But are our sentiments always a threat? Should the emotional part of our personhood always be approached with suspicion? Could our sentiments ever be a good thing?

> "I don't ask you to take away my feelings, Lord, because I can use them to serve you: but I ask you to put them through the crucible."
> —ST. JOSEMARÍA ESCRIVÁ

Morally Neutral

As human beings, we possess a body and a spiritual soul. Our spiritual soul distinguishes us from the animals. The animals, having only a material soul in the context of a "life force," live by instinct. Although they can be conditioned by training and rewards, they are creatures of base impulses. For example, a dog will never stop and pray and reflect on whether it should bite someone it doesn't know. As human beings, we also possess instincts, but our spiritual souls allow us to transcend, order, and redirect them for a greater good.

Our spiritual souls consist of our intellect and will. Our intellect allows us to reason and make rational decisions, while our will allows us to exercise prudence, to choose good over evil or a greater good over a lesser good, and to structure the abilities of our personhood toward a set decision.

Our feelings and emotions are born from our body or from our body and soul. We can feel hot or cold, as well as have emotions such as euphoria, sorrow, fear, agony, and embarrassment. Since our feelings and emotions are fluid and inconsistent, they have no moral identity. Feeling one way, or having an emotion the other way, can sometimes be beyond our control.

Of themselves, our feelings and emotions have no moral status (CCC 1767). This means that they are neither good nor bad. They are morally neutral. This is an important point!

Our sentiment—the combined experience of our feelings and emotions—cannot be used as a gauge for whether something is good or evil. Our sentiment is not a moral equivalent to the Ten Commandments. Simply that we feel something does not make it right (or wrong).

The moral neutrality of our sentiment, however, does not rest in a vacuum. We experience our feelings and emotions in a real world. This means we often feel them within a particular state of affairs. In light of this reality, what we do with our sentiments determines their moral status. Our feelings and emotions do not simply float away.

Even if we repress or deny them, we will express our feelings and emotions in one way or another, and it is exactly how we manifest them that will decide whether they are morally good or not (CCC 1768, 1774).

For example, if I'm walking into my parish church for worship and a parishioner stops me in the parking lot and lets me have it for something he doesn't like, I can experience anger. The anger has no moral identity yet. If I walk into the church and vent my anger through unkindness to the ushers because of some misplaced object in the narthex, then my anger has become sinful. But if I walk into the church and channel my anger into extra warmth, and a willingness to put misplaced objects in their proper place, then my anger has become virtuous. Our actions and responses determine the moral status of our sentiment.

As we understand sentiment in this way, we can begin to realize the importance of discipline and a moral formation of our hearts. Our intellect and will assist us in the formation our hearts. They provide us with a healthy suspicion of our emotions. Our intellect convicts our sentiment of lies or exaggerations, as our will disciplines and directs our sentiment to a greater good. In order to live free and abundant lives, therefore, we need to accept such a schooling and mentoring of our sentiment so as to live a life of virtue and holiness (John 10:10; Gal. 5:1, 16–26).

Since we are a fallen people—created good but inclined to sin—if we are devoid of a moral compass, our sentiments will demand to be worshipped and obeyed. They will overwhelm our hearts and lead us into a profound darkness. Our sentiments cannot stand alone.

As Christian believers and people of goodwill, we realize that we must work to order and direct our sentiments so they will match the sentiments and way of life of the Lord Jesus (see Phil. 2:5; CCC 1769–1770). We labor in this effort so that we might possess the full maturity, the full stature, of Jesus Christ (Eph. 4:13). If our sentiments seek to lead us astray, they must be disciplined and brought into alignment with moral goodness (Rom. 13:13–14). If our sentiments are wounded and incline us toward malicious actions, they must be healed and channeled into positive and uplifting actions (1 Pet. 2:24).

As our sentiments are guided by moral truth, they are dethroned from any misplacement in our hearts and placed in their proper place in our lives. We are called to form our consciences, to build up the moral strength of our hearts, to exercise a robust virtue of religion, and so to worthily worship the living God.

With this explanation of sentiment in mind, questions arise. Does sentiment have a place in worship? If yes, what does worship look like when sentiment is welcomed?

> **"Do not be guided by feeling,
> because it is not always under your control;
> but all merit lies in the will."**
> **—THE LORD JESUS TO ST. FAUSTINA**

Positive Place

As a college student, I attended Franciscan University of Steubenville. That university has been influenced by the Catholic Charismatic Renewal. As a young person coming from the South and from a military family, I was caught off guard by the charged use of the emotions at the many prayer opportunities on campus. As I made a circle of friends who were more familiar or comfortable with such emotional expressions, I found myself more open to such an expression. And I was amazed by the conversion, healing, and deeper conviction that happened within me.

The Franciscan University follows a method of "dynamic orthodoxy." It calls the student body to a relationship with Jesus Christ and to a love for the Church and its worship. It acknowledges our modern culture and employs a heavy use of the emotions in order to engage students and provoke them to an ever deepening following of Jesus Christ.

In a culture where emotions have become king, and sentiment is the rule of the day, it's a prudent and strategic evangelization method. It acknowledges the good of our emotive selves and directs it, through prayer and holy fellowship, to a deeper maturity in the Lord Jesus. And so it's no surprise that many upper classmen tend to replace, or parallel, the praise and worship sessions (with their strong use of emotions) with adoration of the Blessed Sacrament, since the more our emotions mature, the less inclined they are to external or spirited expression.

Although I do not agree with some of the practices used at Mass, Franciscan University provides many extra-liturgical opportunities for prayer that serve as a positive example of the use of emotions in a program of formation for university students. The emotional expression is placed within the greater work of dynamic orthodoxy, and the emotions are able to lead young people to an acceptance of Jesus Christ and his most excellent way of love. The emotions are not given a license to do whatever they prefer, or a false freedom to define for themselves who God is or what truth is, nor are they left where they are with no sense of direction or calls to greater maturity. The emotions are encouraged but guided and led along the way to an encounter with the true and living God.

The university is a helpful example to see how the emotions can be used well.

Following this example, I think it's important to stress that as we grow older, we are called to a less animated expression of emotion. As we age, our emotions should mature. Any use of emotion should have a greater goal in mind. The emotions should be solicited not only for the sake of soliciting them. They are a means to an end. If used correctly, they can be a powerful means to motivate and inspire faith.

As an example, I would encourage more emotion during the homily and less emotion in the music. The appropriate use of emotion by a homilist can give an impassioned witness to the Lord and call the community of believers to greater faith. Music, however, tends to take on a life of its own. I have found that traditional music, known and sung by the congregation, does more to emotionally direct adult believers to the Lord Jesus. Loud music, multi-instrumental music, and performance-like music tend to distract believers and give too little direction to a focused worship of God. The goal is never an emotional experience for the sake of itself, but always to channel our emotions to a greater good, such as a true worship of God.

Strengthened by these teachings on sentiment, let's evaluate when religion tries to become mere sentiment.

> **"Never exaggerate, but express your feelings with moderation."**
> **—ST. TERESA OF ÁVILA**

Criteria of the Virtue of Religion

Since we've now explored religion as sentiment, let's see how sentiment measures up against the five criteria of the true virtue of religion.

1. *God as God:* When sentiment takes over, it seeks to replace God as God and become a god itself. Our sentiments are fallen. When they are not ordered to God, they seek the worship that is due to him alone.

2. *Humble Recognition:* When sentiment is not ordered by and to truth, there is nothing humble about it. Unruly sentiment is an arrogant spirit that recognizes nothing other than itself and its own satisfaction.

3. *Debt to God:* When religion becomes sentiment, there is no recognized debt to God. Sentiment becomes bloated with entitlement and argues that a debt is owed to itself. Such a wayward sentiment nurtures self-pity and self-victimization.

4. *Gratitude and Obedience:* When religion becomes sentiment, there is no gratitude to God or anyone else. There is no recognized truth beyond itself and, therefore, no obedience to anything other than its own whims and pleasure.

5. *Connection to Others:* Absolutized sentiment has no connection to anyone. It creates its own small world and dwells in that dark place. It becomes its own god and has no room for love of God or neighbor.

In the above assessment, we see the dangers and tragedies that occur when religion becomes sentiment. In recognizing such dangers, we need to examine when and how such overtures have entered into our own exercise of the virtue of religion. The following *Application to Our Lives* will assist us in this review.

> "Christian morality does not regard human feelings with distrust. On the contrary, it gives importance to fostering and guiding them, since they have a great bearing on living a happy life."
> —ST. JOSEMARÍA ESCRIVÁ

Application to Our Lives

Examination of conscience

The following questions are meant as a help in examining our own consciences on the virtue of religion and the worship of God:

- Do I have a healthy suspicion of my emotions and acknowledge that the way I feel is not always reality?

- Do I allow my sentiment to change my understanding of God?

- Do I regularly participate in Mass and allow the Church's prayers to mold and shape my own prayers?

- Do I accept the power of God's grace, even if I don't feel it?

- Have I overreacted to a biblical teaching that challenges how I feel about something?

- Do I show a docile and open spirit to divine revelation and the Church's teachings on God and true worship?

- Have I indulged in distracting and/or self-focused aspects of worship?

- Do I pray even when I don't feel like it?

- When my emotions are provoked, do I pause and allow my intellect and will to inform and order them for a greater good?

- Do I periodically laugh at myself and the fluidity of emotions that pass through my heart?

Having made this examination of conscience, it is recommended that you go and make a good confession based on these points.

Pointers for apologetics

As a help in speaking to our fellow believers and to unbelievers around us, here are some pointers for apologetics:

1. As human beings, we possess a body and soul. Our spiritual souls consist of our intellect and will. Our sentiments—feelings and emotions—are fluid and do not have a moral identity by themselves.

2. The moral status of our sentiments is based on what we do with them. Depending on how we act, our sentiments can be morally good or evil.

3. How we feel is not always reality.

4. Simply because we feel something, that does not mean it is morally acceptable.

5. The best help to the formation of our hearts, and the guiding of our sentiment, is the virtue of religion and the true worship of God.

Key points

Having the pointers for apologetics as a foundation, we can now stress some key points from this chapter:

- Since sentiment is not always reality, we must rely on reality to guide our sentiments.

- If sentiment is not directed by a well formed heart, then it will follow the waywardness of our human fallenness.

- When sentiment follows our fallenness, it will create its own reality and manipulate our views of God and truth in order to accommodate its own whims, pleasures, and worldview.

- In such a fallen state, our sentiment will demand to be worshipped and obeyed. It will seek to replace the true God.

- When sentiment replaces God, then religion ceases to be a virtue. In such a case, religion becomes sentiment, and we end up worshipping only ourselves.

Devotional exercise

St. Teresa's Bookmark

Let nothing disturb you,
Let nothing frighten you,
All things pass away:
God never changes.
Patience obtains all things.
He who has God
Finds he lacks nothing;
God alone suffices.

Litany of Humility

O Jesus! meek and humble of heart, Hear me.
From the desire of being esteemed,

- *Deliver me, Jesus.*
  [repeat after each line]
From the desire of being loved,
From the desire of being extolled,
From the desire of being honored,
From the desire of being praised,
From the desire of being preferred to others,
From the desire of being consulted,
From the desire of being approved,
From the fear of being humiliated,
From the fear of being despised,
From the fear of suffering rebukes,
From the fear of being calumniated,

From the fear of being forgotten,
From the fear of being ridiculed,
From the fear of being wronged,
From the fear of being suspected,
That others may be loved more than I,

* *Jesus, grant me the grace to desire it.*
   [repeat after each line]
That others may be esteemed more than I ,
That, in the opinion of the world,
others may increase and I may decrease,
That others may be chosen and I set aside,
That others may be praised and I unnoticed,
That others may be preferred to me in everything,
That others may become holier than I,
provided that I may become as holy as I should.

Act of Faith
O my God, I firmly believe
that you are one God in three divine Persons,
Father, Son, and Holy Spirit.
I believe that your divine Son became man
and died for our sins and that he will come
to judge the living and the dead.
I believe these and all the truths
which the Holy Catholic Church teaches
because you have revealed them
who are eternal truth and wisdom,

who can neither deceive nor be deceived.
In this faith I intend to live and die.
Amen.

Stations of the Cross

As you pray the stations of the cross, ask for the grace to avoid the excess of sentiment in the virtue of religion. In particular, focus on the eighth station, when Jesus admonishes the weeping women: "Daughters of Jerusalem, do not weep for me, but weep for yourselves and for your children. For behold, the days are coming when they will say, 'Blessed are the barren, and the wombs that never bore, and the breasts that never gave suck!' Then they will begin to say to the mountains, 'Fall on us'; and to the hills, 'Cover us.' For if they do this when the wood is green, what will happen when it is dry?"

—LUKE 23:28-31

Rosary Suggestions

When praying the mysteries of the rosary, consider these various points:

Joyful Mysteries: The discipline of the Holy Family, whose members ordered their emotions and desires so as to accomplish all that was asked of them.

Luminous Mysteries: The sense of mission that marked the public ministry of the Lord Jesus, as he directed his entire human nature—sentiments and all—to the accomplishment of the Father's will.

Sorrowful Mysteries: The extreme ordering of the Lord Jesus' entire human nature—including his emotions—to the messianic mission given to him, and his total willingness to accept suffering out of his love for the Father and humanity.

Glorious Mysteries: The great joy that awaits us in eternity as we imitate the Lord Jesus in his loving obedience and sense of mission.

Guardian Angel Prayer
Angel of God, my guardian dear,
to whom God's love commits me here,
Ever this day be at my side, to light and guard,
to rule and guide. Amen.

WHEN RELIGION BECOMES SELF-HELP

I say to the Lord, "Thou art my Lord;
I have no good apart from thee."

—Psalm 16:2

It's an odd observation to see so many people in Western culture so obsessed with themselves, all the while thinking they are somehow improving themselves or growing toward some state of perfection. It's not uncommon to hear about the latest diet, meditative experience, or work-out. People have created an entire culture that revolves around themselves and a self-focused regimen of personal health.

Some time ago, in a previous pastoral assignment, I met with a young man who showed me his daily schedule. He was proud of the balance he had achieved among his work, exercise, dietary restrictions, entertainment and social activities, and religious observance. I was impressed as he presented his schedule and explained the discipline required to keep it, but I was also concerned. In listening to his talk for over thirty minutes, it appeared that his true god was his own method of self-help and the supposed balance he achieved through his own efforts.

In such a way of life, his "religious observance" (as he called it) seemed to be just one more thing on his schedule and list of goals. Now, I was happy to see that religious observance had made the list, and I'm aware that for many young people, it's not even in the arena. But there was a misperception in where it was and how it was being approached. And so, a conversation ensued.

I asked the young man, "Now, tell me, what do you mean by 'religious observance'?" He seemed confused as to why I wouldn't know what he meant. After a few seconds, he responded, "Well, you know, Father—go to Mass and follow a schedule of prayers."

"Great," I said, "and does religious observance mean anything else? Maybe some aspects of virtue or service to the poor?"

"Yes," he said quickly. "I have those under social activities and service projects."

"Okay, wonderful," I said. "Do you think 'religious observance' is the best possible term to use? Do you think it makes your discipleship sound like just one more thing to do, rather than the heart and purpose of everything you do?"

I could tell by his facial expression that I was turning his world upside-down, so I wanted to give some more clarity and explanation. "What I mean is that as Christians, our discipleship and call to worship is the center of our lives. It's what everything else revolves around. It's not just one more thing on our list of 'to do' items. Does that make sense?"

"Yes, Father," he responded, "but I know that. I'm just trying to get everything on my schedule that I want to do and should do to live a good . . . you know, balanced life."

"I can see that," I elaborated, "and I'm impressed. You've put some hard work into your schedule and desire for balance. But what's your response if God is asking you do something that might bring imbalance to your life? As Christians, we know that sometimes God asks us to sacrifice good things in our service to him and our neighbor. Do you see that nuance and why it's really important?"

The conversation went on for a little while longer and ended well. He was a good person who wanted to do the right things in life. I'm confident that God will guide him along the adventurous path of generous discipleship.

In many respects, he was an accentuated example of the many people in our culture who have created a pseudo-religion of self-help. They have orchestrated a life centered on personal growth and self-actualization. Self-actualization as a goal solely unto itself becomes an idol. Any desire for personal growth needs the demands of the virtue of religion and the summons to true worship, since these are the principal means by which we come to know who we are and what we are called to become.

We cannot attempt to hijack religion and turn it into just one more thing to somehow make us better people. Such a confusion of priorities indicates a lack of virtue in terms of religion and worship.

This reality in our culture raises a few questions. How do we understand the virtue of religion in our lives? Has it become a passive "religious observance" that's only a part of an overall list of some form of self-help? Have we allowed the call to worship to be subordinated to some other goal other than the adoration of God and the death of ourselves in service to him and our neighbor?

Life Coach from on High

Although the desire to improve our lives and grow in self-possession can be an admirable thing in and of itself, when it becomes our religion, we focus on ourselves—what we can get or become—rather than on God and our call to offer him true adoration and self-emptying glorification. Our self-possession should always be focused on self-donation and self-oblation. We possess ourselves so that we have something to give God and others. Our desire for self-improvement, and for a greater self-possession, should never be an end in itself.

When self-help becomes our religion, God becomes a mere means or instrument to make our lives more holistic, enriched, or meaningful. Such a rapport doesn't reflect the approach of a creature turning toward its Creator, or a creature-turned-child addressing its heavenly Father. Rather, it resembles a client making demands of a life coach and expecting some self-desired results.

True religion, however, is not about self-actualization, our success, our self-esteem, or self-optimization. Rather, it is about a poverty of spirit, a crucified love, a self-emptying, and a meekness that allows the human heart to know of its dependency on God, and so to yearn for him and truly worship him in spirit and truth.

The sham of self-help religion expects nothing from its pseudo-worshippers other than what they want for themselves. Self-help is an arrogant spirit that insists that the world work for it, go its way, and revolve around its wishes. Such a belief deludes us into presuming that because we are trying to better ourselves, the world should comply with demands to control its ways and means. Self-help religion traps us in a well disguised prison cell of narcissism. It deceives us into creating our own little bubble and dwelling there, focusing only on ourselves, and perceiving the world and those around us as a utilitarian means to our own betterment.

This approach to life and worship is a far cry from the witness given to us by the holy ones in salvation history. The holy ones understood that the only authentic way to personal growth was to forget themselves and focus on the work of God. By putting their efforts into doing God's work, they were able to focus on their interior work. Only by surrendering themselves, wholly and completely to God, did they fully become themselves.

As Pope St. John Paul II wrote in his encyclical *Redemptor Hominis* (The Redeemer of Man):

> The man who wishes to understand himself thoroughly— and not just in accordance with immediate, partial, often superficial, and even illusory standards and measures of his being—he must with his unrest, uncertainty and even his weakness and sinfulness, with his life and death, draw near to Christ (10).

This reality was played out in the life of the great apostle, St. Paul. When he was knocked down and called by the Lord Jesus (Acts 9:4, 15–16), he accepted the call and offered himself as a libation to God's service (Acts 9:18–19; 2 Tim. 4:6). Although the worst of all sinners, he gave his entire life—as broken as it was—as a priestly service for the proclamation of the gospel (Rom. 15:16; 1 Tim. 1:15). The great saint didn't plan a self-help program to get his life together. Paul offered himself as a sacrifice and let God do the interior work in his soul that needed to be done, as he would say:

> For what we preach is not ourselves, but Jesus Christ as Lord, with ourselves as your servants for Jesus' sake. . . . But we have this treasure in earthen vessels, to show that the transcendent power belongs to God and not to us (2 Cor. 4:5, 7).

Paul held no delusions of himself, or of any help that he could give to himself. He realized how much he truly needed the Lord Jesus and the workings of his grace. As he wrote:

> But by the grace of God I am what I am, and his grace toward me was not in vain. On the contrary, I worked harder than any of them, though it was not I, but the grace of God which is with me (1 Cor. 15:10).

Further, he writes:

> But whatever gain I had, I counted as loss for the sake of Christ. Indeed I count everything as loss because of the surpassing worth of knowing Christ Jesus my Lord. For his sake I have suffered the loss of all things, and count them as refuse, in order that I may gain Christ (Phil. 3:7–8).

And so, we see a completely different approach from Paul, and the many holy ones described throughout salvation history. This witness convicts our culture of its obsession with itself and redirects us to a different way of life.

If we desire to be fully alive, we must become an acceptable sacrifice (Rom. 12:1–2). Rather than focusing on ourselves and our needs, we are summoned to hear the call of the gospel, to offer ourselves as an oblation in true worship, and to take up our cross and follow the Lord Jesus (Matt. 10:38). If we follow such a way, the Lord promises us: "For whoever would save his life will lose it, and whoever loses his life for my sake will find it" (Matt. 16:25).

Paul, the apostle to the Gentiles, admonishes us to abandon our vanities and the follies of this world and to follow a Christ-centered way of life. He gives the following exhortation:

> I appeal to you therefore, brethren, by the mercies of God, to present your bodies as a living sacrifice, holy and acceptable to God, which is your spiritual worship. Do not be conformed to this world but be transformed by the renewal of your mind, that you may prove what is the will of God, what is good and acceptable and perfect (Rom. 12:1–2).

And so, the path of self-help is futile. It leads only to self-absorption, delusion, denial, and isolation. It leads us into a veiled self-pity and a wayward sense of entitlement. Worst of all, it's a display of pride, since it manipulates itself to appear as a noble thing, when in reality it is only idolatry and self-worship.

As the children of God, who are called to exercise the virtue of religion and to worship God alone, we must avoid allowing self-help to become a false religion in our lives. We must stay focused on the true and living God and become a living sacrifice, accepting and exploring every opportunity to worthily worship him and selflessly serve him. Our attention must be on God. Our growth and personal development are good things of themselves, but they can never eclipse or overshadow the virtue of religion or the worship of the true God. God in all his majesty is not a means or an instrument to anything else. He is not a life coach from on high. He is the All-Powerful, Ever-Living, Ancient of Days, the Alpha and Omega. And he calls us—not only to worship, but to be the fragrant holocaust of worship, pleasing to him.

What does it mean to be an oblation to God? With our sinful hearts, can we offer a worthy sacrifice to him? How can we present ourselves, fallen and wayward, to the all-holy God? How can our sacrifice be acceptable to him?

> "Cling to God and leave all the rest to him: he will not let you perish. Your soul is very dear to him, he wishes to save it."
>
> —ST. MARGARET MARY ALACOQUE OF THE SACRED HEART

The Transformative Power of Worship

If the average Catholic were to be asked, "In the Mass, are we in the Upper Room or at Calvary?" the majority would answer, "In the Upper Room." Such an answer would be so incomplete as to be wrong. The lack of knowledge on the nature of the Mass has contributed to a mistaken view of worship. If worship, which is the highest function of the human person, becomes mere table fellowship, in which nothing is given, nothing is sacrificed, and everyone is welcome with no expectation of repentance and transformation, then the work of religion—the real conversion of the human person—will be sought and pursued elsewhere.

It is an interesting phenomenon that those who complain about "the rules" of the Church are oftentimes the same ones who impose immense rules upon themselves for self-improvement. Such people reject weekly Mass but will not skip a day at the gym. They will reject the eucharistic fast but fast excessively for weight loss. They will refuse to go to confession but will sit in hours of therapy confessing their sins or lounge in a sauna or some other type of treatment to purge their bodies and focus their minds. When the demands of true religion are placed alongside the demands of self-help, it's clear that the rules and disciplines are not the problem, since such practices are accepted and lived out for personal development. The problem is that the person is choosing these practices in order to serve only himself rather than God.

Perhaps, therefore, a review and restoration of the nature of the Mass can help us. If we are called to be a living sacrifice, how can this sacrifice be made, and how can this sacrifice be acceptable to God? The answers to these and similar questions are found in the proper understanding of the Mass.

Every baptized person is a member of the body of Christ. Membership here is not akin to a club membership with a card and group privileges. The membership here is in reference to the parts of a body (Rom. 12:4–5), as we would speak of someone who has lost an arm as being *dismembered*. As parts of the body of Christ, we share in the work of Jesus Christ, and this includes his worship and adoration of God the Father.

The one, historical sacrifice of Jesus Christ was offered 2,000 years ago on Calvary. Because the priest, altar, and victim were God, that sacrifice can continue to be offered for our salvation throughout history until the Lord Jesus returns in glory.

As Ven. Fulton Sheen described the Mass, it's like radio waves. They're running and all around us. But it's only when we turn on the radio that we can hear them. In a similar way, the sacrifice of the Lord Jesus runs through history. When we participate in the Mass, we click on to the sacrifice and are sacramentally present there at Calvary.

As a help in realizing this truth, theology has given us the word *re-present*. At Mass, by the power of the Holy Spirit, the Lord's one, historical sacrifice is *re-presented* for us in an unbloody manner. The baptized who participate in the Mass, therefore, have the immense opportunity to be united with Jesus Christ. In their union with him during the Mass, they are able to offer themselves to the Father "through, with, and in" Jesus Christ. In Christ, therefore, the sacrifice of ourselves to God is possible, and it becomes acceptable in Christ alone. This is the power of the Mass.

By comprehending the nature of the Mass, we can realize what's at stake in the exercise of religion and in the true worship of God. The biblical mandate to be an oblation, a libation, and a living sacrifice to God takes on a practical application in our lives as we realize fully what we are called to do and surrender to God. By offering such true worship, we take the focus off ourselves and redirect it to God.

As we offer true sacrificial worship, and our narcissism and obsession with self-help are dethroned, our world opens up and broadens. We begin to understand our communion with all other believers, living and dead. In the Mass, and by the living out of our baptism, we become spiritually aware of the entire Church in heaven, in Purgatory, and throughout the world.

We grasp more fully what St. Paul taught: "There is one body and one Spirit, just as you were called to the one hope that belongs to your call, one Lord, one faith, one baptism, one God and Father of us all, who is above all and through all and in all" (Eph. 4:4–6).

This truth is expressed in our response to the priest's invitation: "Pray, brothers and sisters, that my sacrifice and yours may be acceptable to God, the almighty Father." We say, "May the Lord accept the sacrifice at your hands for the praise and glory of his name, for our good and the good of all his holy Church."

In this simple response, we see four petitions. We ask that our sacrifice (united to Christ's) may be acceptable. From there, we ask that our modest sacrifice might give praise and glory to God (not to us). Then we ask that it might be for our good (our true, spiritual well-being), and lastly that it might help the entire holy Church, to which we are united and in communion. These are four truly noble and beautiful aspirations born from real worship of the living God.

And so, infinitely higher and of far greater benefit than any self-help, the Mass and the true worship of God lift us up, heal us, empower us, and direct us along the most excellent way of love (see 1 Cor. 12:31, 15:10; 2 Cor. 12:9–10).

As we desire to offer true worship, there are some dangers in our society. The self-help culture has many masks. There is one in particular that must be exposed and prevented from entering our hearts. It is the popular fallacy of the "best version of myself." What is this fallacy, and why is it so dangerous? How can we avoid it?

> "Often during Mass, I see the Lord in my soul; I feel his presence which pervades my being. I sense his divine gaze; I have long talks with him without saying a word; I know what his divine heart desires, and I always do what will please him the most. I love him to distraction, and I feel that I am being loved by God. At those times, when I meet with God deep within myself, I feel so happy that I do not know how to express it."
>
> —ST. FAUSTINA

The Fallacy of "Best Version of Myself"

The fallacy of the "best version of myself" has received a wide audience and acceptance, even among some good Catholic writers and speakers. But the acceptance of such a fallacy comes at a tremendous price. As fallen human beings, we are inclined to self-love. We must constantly fight that inclination by the practices of true religion and the workings of God's grace in forming virtue in our hearts.

The idea of worshipping God for the sake of getting something out of it, even a better version of ourselves, is the height of arrogance and narcissism. The adoration of God is an end in itself. It can never be used as a means or process to receive something else. We can see the difference between the person who says, "I wish to follow God so I can become the best version of myself" and the person who states, "I wish to follow God because he is God and worthy of my adoration." True worship involves offering empty hands to God as a sign of vulnerability and trust, not as an indication of hope that we'll be given something.

The lie of "best version" feeds off a misunderstanding of the ways of God. In pursuing the path of the Crucified and Risen One, we beg—recalling the declaration of St. John the Baptist—that the Lord Jesus increases, whereas we decrease (John 3:30). In line with such a petition, there will be times in which we are called to surrender portions of ourselves as we follow the Lord Jesus. Similar to Paul's description, there will be moments of exhaustion, poor hygiene, sleep deprivation, financial loss, confusion, relationship problems, betrayal, weight gain, and the list goes on (see 2 Cor. 11:16–33). These are all endured because we love God, we trust him, and we hope to be transformed by his grace in this life, and so be made fit to share eternal life with him (2 Tim. 4:7–8). This is the virtue—the self-forgetfulness—of true religion and the authentic worship of God.

In addition, the "best version" fallacy ignores our call to be a living sacrifice in worship and in our selfless service to our neighbors. The virtue of religion naturally involves a service to the poor, sick, and outcast. It includes a heart for the wayward and lost. In the Christian tradition, such out-reach has been summarized as the works of mercy (see *Devotional exercise* below). In our efforts to exercise the virtue of religion and to grow in holiness, we cannot be navel-gazing, stuck in a paralysis by analysis. We are called to get out of ourselves and to be instruments of love, healing, and peace to those around us.

On this point, Paul is adamant. He writes:

We who are strong ought to bear with the failings of the weak, and not to please ourselves (Rom. 15:1).

Bear one another's burdens, and so fulfil the law of Christ (Gal. 6:2).

Let each of you look not only to his own interests, but also to the interests of others. Have this mind among yourselves, which was in Christ Jesus, who, though he was in the form of God, did not count equality with God a thing to be grasped, but emptied himself, taking the form of a servant, being born in the likeness of men (Phil. 2:4–7).

In this way, we can see more clearly the teachings of the Lord Jesus, especially in terms of our care for those in need. The Lord is stark as he describes our day of judgment. We will not be judged by the best version of ourselves. In fact, our supposed glory may end up being our greatest shame before the throne of our Lord. He will judge us by our acts of love and kindness done in him and by the power of his grace (Matt. 25:31–46). As the Lord Jesus explains the rationale behind his judgment:

> Then the righteous will answer him, "Lord, when did we see thee hungry and feed thee, or thirsty and give thee drink? And when did we see thee a stranger and welcome thee, or naked and clothe thee? And when did we see thee sick or in prison and visit thee?" And the King will answer them, "Truly, I say to you, as you did it to one of the least of these my brethren, you did it to me" (vv. 37–40).

In these ways, the fallacy of the "best version of myself" is unmasked, along with the overall futile effort at self-help. The desire to be a better person and to nurture growth and development within us is a noble aspiration, but the virtue of religion is not solely about self-help or self-optimization. The virtue of religion is about a total surrender to God as a living sacrifice to him. It's about focusing on God's kingdom, and not our own, and about a selfless service to those in need.

When we seek God's kingdom first, then all other things will be given to us (Matt. 6:33). The principal question is about priority and intention. We seek God's glory above our own, and then he lifts us up to unimaginable heights. If, however, we seek only ourselves and such glory—and use God as a mere means—then we have reversed the true priority and adulterated the right intention, and we have turned a blessing into a curse.

The Lord Jesus describes the proper priority of discipleship and worship:

> For whoever would save his life will lose it, and whoever loses his life for my sake will find it. For what will it profit a man if he gains the whole world and forfeits his life? Or what shall a man give in return for his life? (Matt. 16:25–26).

Our focus, therefore, must be God alone. Our worship is about him and not the blessings we receive from him. As St. Teresa of Ávila taught us: "We worship the God of consolation, not the consolations of God."

Strengthened by these teachings on self-help, let's evaluate when religion tries to become solely an exercise in self-help.

> "Love cannot remain by itself—it has no meaning. Love has to be put into action, and that action is service."
> —ST. TERESA OF CALCUTTA

Criteria of the Virtue of Religion

Since we've now explored religion as self-help, let's see how self-help efforts measure up against the five criteria of the true virtue of religion.

1. *God as God:* When self-help becomes our focus, it overtakes our desire to grow in our relationship with God. It replaces a pursuit of holiness with empty goals of self-enrichment. Self-help blinds us to our narcissism and convinces us that our efforts at self-improvement are noble, when they really only self-worship.

2. *Humble Recognition:* When self-help becomes our religion, it's an arrogant spirit. Our attention is only on ourselves and our desires for self-growth. Self-help is marked by pride and refuses to give any recognition to God, other than as a mere means to achieving personal accolades.

3. *Debt to God:* When religion becomes self-help, there is no acknowledged debt. We become self-absorbed and seek our personal optimization. Self-help falsely believes that God owes us a debt. He must play his part in making us better people.

4. *Gratitude and Obedience:* When religion becomes self-help, gratitude disappears and is replaced by a raw sense of entitlement. There is no obedience other than to oneself. God is discreetly replaced by ourselves, and we become the sole recipients of any spiritual goods or acts of worship.

5. *Connection to Others:* Self-help by its name dismisses the other. There is no connection to other people beyond utility. People are used as a means to gain something for ourselves.

In the above assessment, we see the dangers and tragedies that occur when religion becomes self-help. In recognizing such dangers, we need to examine when and how such overtures have entered into our own exercise of the virtue of religion. The following *Application to Our Own Lives* will assist us in this review.

> **"Put all the good works in the world against one Holy Mass; they will be as a grain of sand beside a mountain."**
> **—ST. JOHN VIANNEY**

Application to Our Lives

Examination of conscience

The following questions are meant as a help in examining our own consciences on the virtue of religion and the worship of God:

- Do I approach God only when I want something?

- Is the exercise of religion just one more thing in my life, or does it hold my entire heart?

- Throughout my day, do I talk more to God or to myself?

- Do I understand the nature of the Mass and actively participate in it?

- Have I sought to nurture an awareness of my communion with all believers, living and dead?

- Have I sought to spiritually befriend the saints, especially those who share a vocation, temperament, or spirituality with me?

- Have I subordinated my desires for personal growth to the love and service of God alone?

- Do I try to grasp the meaning of being a "living sacrifice" to God and live this reality throughout my day?

- Have I failed in fulfilling the demands of true religion because of a conflict with personal goals or wishes?

- Do I seek to break my self-centeredness by actively focusing on the needs of my neighbor?

Having made this examination of conscience, it is recommended that you go and make a good confession based on these points.

Pointers for apologetics

As a help in speaking to our fellow believers or to unbelievers around us, here are some pointers for apologetics:

1. God alone is worthy to be praised and worshipped. Self-help deceives us and puts our attention only on ourselves.

2. Self-help of itself can be a noble effort, but it oftentimes oversteps its boundaries and becomes a pseudo-religion.

3. When self-help takes over our lives, God is eclipsed.

4. Self-help deludes us and leads us into disguised narcissism and self-worship.

5. Self-help denies the value of anything beyond its own efforts.

Key points

Having the pointers for apologetics as a foundation, we can now stress some key points from this chapter:

• Self-help can be a good thing, but our nature is fallen, and it oftentimes leads to self-worship.

• Self-help worsens when true worship is absent.

• The holy sacrifice of the Mass is the greatest destroyer of misplaced self-help, since it leads the believer into a self-oblation before the living God.

- The communion of saints exposes the isolation of a self-help pseudo-religion.

- A selfless service to those in need, expressed in the works of mercy, is a great help in breaking any egoism caused by a self-help mentality.

Devotional exercise

Suscipe **Prayer**

Take, O Lord,
and receive my entire liberty,
my memory, my understanding,
and my whole will.
All that I am and all that I possess,
You have given me:
I surrender it all to you
to be disposed of according to your will.
Give me only your love and your grace;
with these I will be rich enough
and will desire nothing more.
Amen.

Works of Mercy

Corporal:
Feed the hungry
Give drink to the thirsty
Shelter the homeless
Clothe the naked

Visit the sick
Visit the imprisoned
Bury the dead

Spiritual:
Instruct the ignorant
Counsel the doubtful
Admonish the sinner
Forgive injuries
Comfort the sorrowful
Bear wrongs patiently
Pray for the living and dead

Act of Faith
O my God, I firmly believe
that you are one God in three divine Persons,
Father, Son, and Holy Spirit.
I believe that your divine Son became man
and died for our sins and that he will come
to judge the living and the dead.
I believe these and all the truths
which the Holy Catholic Church teaches
because you have revealed them
who are eternal truth and wisdom,
who can neither deceive nor be deceived.
In this faith I intend to live and die.
Amen.

Stations of the Cross
As you pray the stations of the cross, ask for the grace to avoid the excess of self-help in the virtue of religion. In particular, focus on the fifth station, when Simon of Cyrene carries the cross for the Lord Jesus. Reflect on Jesus' desire to help you carry the cross and receive its graces: "And they compelled a passer-by, Simon of Cyre'ne, who was coming in from the country, the father of Alexander and Rufus, to carry his cross."
—MARK 15:21

Rosary Suggestions

When praying the mysteries of the rosary, consider these various points:

Joyful Mysteries: The utter docility and reliance of the Holy Family upon the power and favor of God the Father.

Luminous Mysteries: The communion and trust of the Lord Jesus toward the Father throughout his public ministry.

Sorrowful Mysteries: The trust and selfless love of the Lord Jesus for the Father throughout his dolorous passion.

Glorious Mysteries: The communion among the Father, the Son, and the Holy Spirit. The eternal confidence of our Lady in the will of God.

Guardian Angel Prayer
Angel of God, my guardian dear,
to whom God's love commits me here,
Ever this day be at my side, to light and
guard, to rule and guide. Amen.

4

WHEN RELIGION BECOMES A COMMODITY

Thou hast multiplied, O Lord my God,
thy wondrous deeds and thy thoughts toward us;
none can compare with thee!
Were I to proclaim and tell of them,
they would be more than can be numbered.

—Psalm 40:5

Some time ago, a married couple with young children reached out and asked if they could come and meet with me. Although I didn't recognize their names, and they weren't in our parish database system, I was happy to make some time to sit down and talk with them.

The conversation started quickly, as the husband and wife wanted to tell me their story and what brought them to my office. Long story short, they were relatively new to the area, had moved here because of work, and had been visiting the local parishes. After the background information, the couple asked me about parish social events, children's programs, family outreach, and other services and resources of the parish. Initially, I was encouraged by their questions and was pleased to describe the opportunities within my parish.

As the conversation continued, however, I began to realize that the young couple and I weren't on the same footing. My description of the parish was an elaboration of a community of disciples of Jesus Christ and the ways in which we seek to follow the gospel way of life. Our programs and services are born from a shared faith and sense of mission. As I spoke with this young couple, the questions and points of interest on their part were indicating a different emphasis.

It became clear to me that this husband and wife weren't searching for a community of faith and conviction in the gospel. They were shopping, and they had a set shopping list. Whereas I was describing a community of faith, they were approaching the parish as if it were only one of many department stores. Rather than seeing the parish's life as an extension of the life lived by the Lord Jesus and the early Church and a call to holy fellowship, they saw the parish in terms of a commodity—a retail approach.

It was a shock when I came to the awareness that these two were actually interviewing me, assessing whether my parish was up to their commercial demands. If we didn't have the programs and resources the couple were looking for, then they were going to move on to another parish (or even to a community outside the Catholic Church). It was all about what they could get from the parish.

This is the tragic state of religion when it becomes a cold commodity. The focus becomes what we can receive rather than what we can give. We approach God and the Church as if they were merely benefactors responsible for giving us the things we want or prefer. We diminish the all-powerful and ever-living God, and the community of disciples that surround him, into cheap Pez dispensers. In this action, the virtue of religion becomes a mere utility, a means for our use, enjoyment, and pleasure. Worship becomes adulterated and unable to fulfill the call to self-oblation.

This story can be surprising, and even disturbing, especially if we ask ourselves some hard questions. Do we approach God as if he were only some divine handyman who is to serve us and fulfill our wants and demands? Do we expect the Church to be stripped of her richness and become a meager opportunity for recreation and social interaction?

Do we attempt to deplete true worship of its power and grace and turn it into a soulless community gathering, a sad concert of self-focused songs, or a collection of cheap theatrics for personal amusement? Will we name this false spirit of commodity and labor for the true virtue of religion in our lives?

> "There is no place for selfishness and no place for fear! Do not be afraid, then, when love makes demands. Do not be afraid when love requires sacrifice."
>
> —POPE ST. JOHN PAUL II

The Gospel, Not a Garage Sale

In the fullness of time, God sent his Son among us (Gal. 4:4). In his life and ministry, Jesus Christ fulfilled all the prophecies and promises of God contained in the Old Testament. In this action, he showed himself to be the fulfillment of all revelation. In Jesus Christ, humanity has received the entirety of all revelation. God the Father has spoken all that he wishes to say in and through his Son, the Word made flesh.

> And the Word became flesh and dwelt among us, full of grace and truth; we have beheld his glory, glory as of the only Son from the Father (John 1:14).

In giving us his revelation, the Lord Jesus has provided us with the full message of salvation. He has shown us the face of our Father and modeled for us the most excellent way of love.

For those men and women, who acknowledge and believe in his revelation, and accept the call to follow him, they see Jesus Christ as the Son of God, Messiah, and Lord:

> Simon Peter replied, "You are the Christ, the Son of the living God" (Matt. 16:16).

> Thomas answered him, "My Lord and my God!" (John 20:28).

> And every tongue confess that Jesus Christ is Lord, to the glory of God the Father (Phil. 2:11).

In accepting the call to follow, such disciples choose to truly follow him. They heard the call: "And he said to them, 'Follow me, and I will make you fishers of men,'" and surrendered everything to him (Matt. 4:19). They do not attempt a rebellion against him. They do not nurture doubt against his way of life. They do not claim a false enlightenment that places them above his teachings or those of his Church. They do not reject Jesus Christ by offering false or wayward worship.

Such men and women are disciples. They are captivated by the Lord's love and mercy, and they seek nothing other than to unconditionally reciprocate his love, faithfully follow him, and allow his grace to transform them and make them fit for his heavenly kingdom. Within the realm of all public revelation, they also see the Lord Jesus as the personal fulfillment of all their own hopes and dreams in this life.

Such disciples aspire to live the prayer of the Prophet Samuel: "Speak, Lord, for thy servant hears" (1 Sam. 3:9–10), rather than regressing and declaring, "Listen up, Lord, your servant is speaking!"

As a part of that personal surrender, the disciple accepts the totality of the teachings of the Lord Jesus with the "obedience of faith" (Rom. 1:5). The disciple asks for the grace to incorporate and integrate the full gospel of Jesus Christ into his life. He rejects any form of idolatry of the heart and eagerly desires to offer true and lasting worship to the Father through Jesus Christ.

The disciple of the Lord Jesus accepts the gospel as the authentic and everlasting word of God. He does not cut up, carve out, or compromise any of the teachings of Jesus Christ. He does not approach the living word as some type of garage sale, in which he browses the various teachings, checking the cost and examining their usefulness to his own life. He does not assess how the teachings of the Lord Jesus might be adjusted to fit into his own home, nor does he determine for himself—as if he were the one leading, rather than following—what is true or false, what is to be believed or doubted, and what will be obeyed or discarded.

And so, the question that makes the difference between the virtue of religion and the false religion of commodity is whether we approach the teachings and worship of Jesus Christ as the gospel for our salvation and that of the whole world, or whether we access them as a garage sale for our own utility and entertainment.

If we choose to follow the virtue of religion and accept the gospel as a lamp unto our feet, what will our lives look like? What are the marks of a Christ-centered community? In such a community, what should our worship seek to accomplish (and not accomplish)?

> "He who wishes for anything but Christ, does not know what he wishes; he who asks for anything but Christ, does not know what he is asking; he who works, and not for Christ, does not know what he is doing."
>
> —ST. PHILIP NERI

The Way

The apostles and early disciples literally walked and lived with the Lord Jesus. Throughout his time with them, the Lord taught, corrected, guided, and modeled a way of life. St. Paul aptly describes this as "a still more excellent way" (1 Cor. 12:31). After the Lord's paschal mystery—that is, his passion, death, and resurrection—the Lord again walked and lived with his apostles and disciples for another forty days. During that time, since they did not previously have the context and could not fully understand his teachings before the paschal mystery—since who could have imagined that the long-awaited Messiah would be God himself and that salvation would come through suffering?—the Lord spent this time with them re-teaching them the truths of the gospel.

After the Lord's ascension into heaven, the apostles and early Christian disciples developed a way of life based on the life they witnessed the Lord living among them. The Lord offered worship to the Father. He prayed frequently, studied Scripture and quoted it as he taught, formed a community, and always sought those who were hurt or rejected. As such, the early Church sought to be a people of worship, prayer, sacred study, and holy fellowship with a service to the poor and needy (Acts 2:42).

This is the way of life of the believer, and it was truly seen as *a way of life*. It was not a removed adherence to beliefs, a search for the best programs and services, or a disinterested focus on service or community life. This perspective is clear in terms of Church history in that before we were called "Christians" (Acts 11:26), we were simply known as members of "the way" (Acts 9:2), since we were following and living the way of the Lord Jesus.

Christian discipleship, therefore, is understood as an extension of the Lord's own way of life and of his work within the human family. Every believer understands that he is a part of the Lord's own continuing mission to glorify the Father and bring salvation to the world. Every parish community shares in this mission and is called—in the long and beautiful line of Sacred Tradition—to continue the way of the Lord Jesus. The way of life of every Christian community, therefore, reflects this reality, and any programs, services, or outreach launched or sustained by it is understood as a help to bring about the Lord's saving work.

In exploring "the way" of the Christian believer and community, we can see the dynamics between worship and belief, belief and behavior, and behavior and selfless service. The priority, however, is always worship. The "breaking of the bread," the earliest biblical name for the holy sacrifice of the Mass, is the "summit and source" of everything else that's involved in the Christian way of life (see Luke 24:30–31). The worship of the community gives order, meaning, and discipline to everything else that it is called to do and that it accomplishes in his name.

The theological expression *lex orandi, lex credendi* is played out in the life of the Christian community, since truly *the law of prayer* gives spirit, structure, and language to the *law of belief.* In addition, the further theological expressions *ortho-doxy* and *orthopraxy* play themselves out as right worship and belief lead to right action (both in a moral way of life and in the service to the poor). In these ways, we see that the Christian community lives a worship-centered way of life. From this central action of the community, its entire way of life finds organization and purpose.

What happens when a Christian community has lost its way? What occurs when religion becomes a commodity? What happens to worship when commodity takes over?

> "Wherever God has put you, that is your vocation. It is not what we do, but how much love we put into it."
> —ST. TERESA OF CALCUTTA

The Prosperity Gospel and the Megachurch Phenomenon

The fullest unhinged example of religion as a commodity is the rather fashionable, modern teaching known as the Prosperity Gospel, as well as the megachurch phenomenon that it seems to create. Although a predominantly Protestant expression, such a view of life has found its way into the hearts and parishes of Catholics.

The Prosperity Gospel exaggerates the temporal blessings of "health and wealth" and gives bloated versions of biblical promises to its adherents. The basic idea is that God wants to bless us in a temporal, even financial, way. We have to be more open to such blessings and claim them as they come. We also have to give support to the celebrity preacher (who is more akin to a motivational speaker) by extensive tithes, gifts, and book and resource purchases.

Even as a preacher of the Prosperity Gospel gains exorbitant wealth, no questions are raised, since his wealth is seen as a divine affirmation of his message and a sign of the wealth that God wants to give to the members of his congregation.

The Prosperity Gospel denies the reality of Christian discipleship. It dismisses the fallenness and suffering of the world and its redemptive value in Jesus Christ. It offends true worship and turns prayer into a casino of bargaining and profiting from God's favor, real or perceived. The Prosperity Gospel sidesteps the dying to self that is a part of Christian community life (see 2 Cor. 12:8–10). It rejects the many blessings of God that are not in the temporal or financial order. It denies the Lord's clear call to selflessly serve the poor and forgotten, who are biblically understood as blessings and special signs of the Lord's presence among us.

In knowing the life of the Lord Jesus, and the cross that he calls his followers to carry, the Prosperity Gospel is certainly religion as a commodity on steroids. It takes the otherwise discreet, veiled intention of a commodity and takes it to the highest possible level (almost of absurdity). Yet it has thousands of adherents, and dozens of supposed ministers have become wealthy, even multi-millionaires, because of it.

In addition, there are some Catholic Christians who have spiritually accepted the message of the Prosperity Gospel. This is expressed in multiple ways, such as interpreting divine promises within exclusively earthly fulfillments, believing that God owes people something for worshipping him, and the denial of the value of the cross and redemptive suffering. These views have sometimes been expressed in Catholic homiletics and liturgical worship. They can be seen when the focus of preaching and of worship ceases to be the adoration and praise of God and instead becomes a series of reminders of what God owes us and how he is expected to deliver in worldly ways.

In whatever tradition it finds itself, the Prosperity Gospel and the entire effort to turn religion into a commodity are a sour domestication of the gospel and its power. This worldview turns the fierce lion of the gospel into a tamed kitten. The gospel and the virtue of religion, however, are not cheap items in a garage sale. The gospel, and the religion it inspires, is the most awesome and life-changing message ever given to humanity. It is more valuable than any program or service. It is larger than any social event. The gospel reveals our life's mission to us. It calls us to the way of the Lord Jesus. It summons us to true worship.

Of the many parts of our discipleship that the Prosperity Gospel dismisses, the role and importance of redemptive suffering are at the top of the list. As such, it's important for us to go deeper into the mystery of uniting our suffering to that of Jesus Christ.

Redemptive Suffering

In the Mass, after the sacrifice has been offered, and the sacrament is shown to the people, the faithful respond, "Lord, I am not worthy that you should enter under my roof, but only say the word, and my soul shall be healed." The prayer is a reflection of the words of the centurion to the Lord Jesus (Matt. 8:8). As such, they are steeped in New Testament theology and worship.

The words of the centurion, and of believers throughout the ages who echo his humble declaration, show an awareness of our need for God's divine assistance. We are broken and fallen. We need healing and cannot give it to ourselves. Only God can lift us up and give us the healing we need. In making this response, we speak not only for ourselves, but for the entire Church. We all need the Lord's mercy and healing. We need his love and tender care.

As a shared need among all believers, the Lord Jesus allows us to be a part of his saving work. He calls us into his own mission of redemption. We are not spectators or mere recipients of his kindness. We are summoned and commissioned to be by his side and to work with him for the salvation of humanity. Of all the ways in which he calls us to labor with him, the one form of outreach that is most often overlooked or avoided is the role and importance of redemptive suffering. Yes, the Lord will ask us to suffer with him for "our good and the good of all his holy Church," as we pray in the Mass.

And so, no discussion of human life would be complete without addressing the full array of suffering, not only within our souls, but also within our bodies, and in the natural world around us. In experiencing the fullness of human life, Jesus Christ understood and accepted all forms of suffering, and he desires to teach humanity the truths and power that can be born from human suffering. As we see in the letter to the Hebrews:

> In the days of his flesh, Jesus offered up prayers and supplications, with loud cries and tears, to him who was able to save him from death, and he was heard for his godly fear. Although he was a son, he learned obedience through what he suffered; and being made perfect he became the source of eternal salvation to all who obey him (5:7–9).

Ever since humanity's fall from grace, suffering has been viewed as an evil in human life. Christian theology has always seen suffering as an evil and as a consequence of the original sin of Adam and Eve.

In taking on our human nature, Jesus Christ accepted the suffering of humanity, body and soul. All of the Lord's sufferings culminated in the cruelty and torture of his passion and the humiliation of his death. In all these sufferings, he chose to accept, enter, and use suffering, which has been such a pivotal dilemma and source of anguish in human history, as the means to manifest his love and self-donation for humanity.

Suffering itself would become the instrument of salvation, as Paul teaches us in the Kenosis Hymn:

Have this mind among yourselves, which was in Christ Jesus, who, though he was in the form of God, did not count equality with God a thing to be grasped, but emptied himself, taking the form of a servant, being born in the likeness of men. And being found in human form he humbled himself and became obedient unto death, even death on the cross. Therefore God has highly exalted him and bestowed on him the name which is above every name, that at the name of Jesus every knee should bow, in heaven and on earth and under the earth, and every tongue confess that Jesus Christ is Lord, to the glory of God the Father (Phil. 2:5–11).

In taking on human suffering, therefore, the Lord Jesus went directly to sin, understood as the source of suffering in human life. In order to take away sin and vanquish its control on humanity, he became sin itself (John 1:29; 2 Cor. 5:21; 1 Pet. 2:24). He sought to destroy this privation of being, and its consequences of suffering and death, from the inside out.

In becoming sin, Jesus Christ took upon himself all the sins of humanity throughout time. He endured the totality of human guilt, shame, alienation, grief, and confusion, and the full panorama of darkness caused by sin.

As Pope St. John Paul II taught in his encyclical *Dives in Misericordia* (Rich in Mercy):

The cross of Christ on Calvary is also a witness to the strength of evil against the very Son of God, against the one who, alone among all the sons of men, was by his nature absolutely innocent and free from sin, and whose coming into the world was untainted by the disobedience of Adam and the inheritance of original sin. And here, precisely in him, in Christ, justice is done to sin at the price of his sacrifice, of his obedience "even to death." He who was without sin, "God made him sin for our sake."

Justice is also brought to bear upon death, which from the beginning of man's history had been allied to sin. Death has justice done to it at the price of the death of the one who was without sin and who alone was able—by means of his own death—to inflict death upon death. In this way the cross of Christ, on which the Son, consubstantial with the Father, renders full justice to God, is also a radical revelation of mercy, or rather of the love that goes against what constitutes the very root of evil in the history of man: against sin and death (8).

The crucible for this radically human endeavor was the Lord's passion, which began in the Garden of Gethsemane. In the garden, as he took upon himself the sins of humanity, the Lord Jesus sweated blood, felt the full isolation caused by sin, and could not raise his eyes to the heavens. In this sacrificial moment, and by the full weight of his passion, death, and resurrection, Jesus Christ proved his association with suffering humanity and began the process that destroyed the power of sin and death.

Jesus Christ stands as an exemplar of what it means to be human and he shows the human family how to live as the children of God. Truly this witness stands as a model of self-donation and self-service to others.

The suffering of the righteous man was foretold by the prophet Isaiah:

He was despised and rejected by men;
a man of sorrows, acquainted with grief;
and as one from whom men hide their faces
he was despised, and we esteemed him not.
Surely he has borne our griefs
and carried our sorrows;
yet we esteemed him stricken,
smitten by God, and afflicted.
But he was wounded for our transgressions,
he was bruised for our iniquities;
upon him was the chastisement that made us whole,
and with his stripes we are healed.
All we like sheep have gone astray;
we have turned every one to his own way;
and the Lord has laid on him
the iniquity of us all (Isa. 53:3–6).

On account therefore of the unique depth of his human experience, Jesus Christ—true God and true man—has complete credibility as the exemplar of what it means to be human. Additionally, his singular experiential knowledge of suffering in soul and body makes him the standard by which all suffering can be known and offered up as an acceptable sacrifice.

In 1981, when I was a child, I remember the news reports that John Paul II had been shot. It was uncertain how serious his wounds were. Hailed as a miracle, the pope survived the point-blank shooting by a professional assassin. However, he had to remain in the hospital. This was a great struggle for a man who was accustomed to being out and about and among the people. And yet, he listened to his doctors and slowly made a recovery. After his healing, he made the poignant observation, "In hospitals, there is a lot of wasted suffering."

The comment reflected biblical teaching. Baptized Christians are empowered and expected to accept suffering and to offer it up in union with the sufferings of Jesus Christ. This understanding is a core part of what it means to follow the Lord Jesus. In a fallen world, there will be suffering. Among a sinful race, there will be evil and darkness. In the face of such difficulties, the believer turns to Jesus Christ and participates in his perfect sacrifice for the redemption of the world. The suffering is also offered up so the believer can find renewed and rejuvenated meaning, purpose, and value in his sorrows and hardships.

If the Christian does not offer up his suffering, then the suffering is "wasted," and darkness wins. John Paul II did not want sin to win, so he offered up his sufferings with Jesus Christ for our conversion and salvation.

As Christians, each of us is called to do no less. We are called to unite our sufferings with those of Christ and to offer them up for our good and the good of all humanity. Paul writes:

Now I rejoice in my sufferings for your sake, and in my flesh I complete what is lacking in Christ's afflictions for the sake of his body, that is, the church (Col. 1:24).

Although the ministry of Jesus Christ destroyed the kingdom of sin and death, the consequences of sin remain in the human experience. The difference is that suffering—although it is an evil caused by original sin—can now become redemptive for the sufferer and the community. Rather than seeing suffering in merely negative terms, the example and ministry of Jesus Christ now show the human family a positive way in which suffering can be seen and accepted in human life.

John Paul II commented on the universal appreciation of the Lord Jesus' suffering:

The suffering Christ speaks in a special way to man, and not only to the believer. The non-believer also will be able to discover in him the eloquence of solidarity with the human lot, as also the harmonious fullness of a disinterested dedication to the cause of man, to truth and to love (*Dives in Misericordia* 7).

Now, in Jesus Christ, suffering can be a source of repentance, purification, goodness, penance, renewal, hope, and empathy for others who are sick or suffering in some way. In the Lord Jesus, who offered his sufferings as a self-oblation and as a means of selfless service, humanity can see suffering as a new way of service to others and as a new means of self-donation and salvation for the whole world.

This is the call to redemptive suffering. It is our inheritance now in the crucified and risen Christ.

The tragedy of the Prosperity Gospel is that it disregards this unique and powerful part of Christian discipleship. It regards any and all suffering as only an evil and falsely as something to which God would never call us. But the true and living God does call us to suffering. He asks us to labor with him for the salvation of our souls and the souls of all. This call to suffering is as much a part of our life with God as temporal blessings and possible financial success.

> **"The truth does not change according to our ability to stomach it."**
> **—FLANNERY O'CONNOR**

Criteria of the Virtue of Religion

Let's now see how commodity measures up against the five criteria of the true virtue of religion.

1. *God as God:* When commodity becomes religion, we replace God with our own preferences and desires. God is removed by our thirst for some type of payback for everything we do, including worship.

2. *Humble Recognition:* Commodity is all about quid pro quo. There is no room for recognition of God in the heart consumed with commodity. It is a proud spirit that doesn't know humility and is inclined to entitlement and anger.

3. *Debt to God:* Commodity ignores any debt to God. It sees everything in terms of what is given and what is owed. Commodity doesn't believe that it owes anything to God. In fact, it falsely believes that God might owe it something.

4. *Gratitude and Obedience:* Commodity refuses any gratitude since everything is tracked and compensated for according to plans and expectations. There is no obedience in commodity. It acknowledges no authority beyond its own machinations.

5. *Connection to Others:* Commodity sees God and other people only as pawns in its overall game. Everyone is a means. There are no meaningful relationships built on love or selfless service.

In the above assessment, we see the dangers and tragedies that occur when religion becomes a commodity. In recognizing such dangers, we need to examine when and how such overtures have entered into our own exercise of the virtue of religion. The following *Application to Our Lives* will assist us in this review.

Application to Our Lives

Examination of conscience

The following questions are meant as a help in examining our own consciences on the virtue of religion and the worship of God:

- Do I approach God with a disinterested heart?

- Do I ask God what he wants from me rather than placing all my demands on him?

- Do I always have ulterior motives whenever I worship God or participate in parish life?

- In my life, am I always focused on what I'm going to get out of something?

- Have I approached the gospel as a garage sale, taking or leaving whatever I want?

- Do I see Jesus Christ as the fulfillment of all my hopes and dreams?

- Have I sought to be a selfless disciple in my service to others?

- Have I ever left a parish because it didn't have the programs or services I wanted?

- Do I understand the central place of worship in my parish community?

- Do I see the poor and forgotten as blessings and opportunities to encounter the Lord Jesus?

Having made this examination of conscience, it is recommended that you go and make a good confession based on these points.

Pointers for apologetics

As a help in speaking to our fellow believers or to unbelievers around us, here are some pointers for apologetics:

1. God cannot be used for any use or means. He is all-holy and is an end in himself.

2. Commodity is offensive to true religion since it focuses on what the worshipper will receive and not on what he is called to give or surrender.

3. Commodity turns the gospel into a garage sale, where self-identified believers pick and choose what they will believe or obey.

4. The "obedience of faith" is a powerful response to remove religion as a commodity from our souls since it

calls for a docile posture before the Lord and his Church.

5. Christian community life and service to those in need are the actions most opposed to commodity.

Key points

Having the pointers for apologetics as a foundation, we can now stress some key points from this chapter:

- Commodity is interested only in what it can get out of something, even worship and discipleship.

- Commodity kills community life and makes the world into one huge quid pro quo.

- The life of the Lord Jesus, and the witness of the early Church, dispels the intrigue of religion as a commodity.

- The holy sacrifice of the Mass is the summit and source of the Christian way of life. It calls the believer to die to himself and his self-interest. It's a powerful cure for religion as a commodity.

- The Prosperity Gospel, and its accompanying megachurch phenomenon, is the most extreme form of religion as a commodity. It is a dangerous and growing reality in our world.

Devotional exercise

Act of Spiritual Communion

My Jesus,

I believe that you are present in the Most Holy Sacrament.
I love you above all things,
and I desire to receive you into my soul.
Since I cannot at this moment receive you sacramentally,
come at least spiritually into my heart.
I embrace you as if you were already there
and unite myself wholly to you.
Never permit me to be separated from you.
Amen.

Prayer of Love of St. John Vianney
I love you, O my God,
and my only desire is to love you until my last breath.
I love you, O infinitely lovable God,
and I prefer to die loving you
rather than to live for a single moment without loving you.
I love you, O my God,
and I long for heaven
only to know the bliss of loving you perfectly.
Amen.

Act of Faith
O my God, I firmly believe
that you are one God in three divine Persons,
Father, Son, and Holy Spirit.
I believe that your divine Son became man
and died for our sins and that he will come
to judge the living and the dead.

I believe these and all the truths
which the Holy Catholic Church teaches
because you have revealed them
who are eternal truth and wisdom,
who can neither deceive nor be deceived.
In this faith I intend to live and die.
Amen.

> ### Stations of the Cross
> As you pray the stations of the cross, ask for the graces to avoid the excesses of commodity in the virtue of religion. In particular, focus on the *first station*, when Pilate, consumed by self-interest and commodity, condemns Jesus to death: "So when Pilate saw that he was gaining nothing, but rather that a riot was beginning, he took water and washed his hands before the crowd, saying, 'I am innocent of this righteous man's blood; see to it yourselves.'"
> —MATT. 27:24

Rosary Suggestions

When praying the mysteries of the rosary, consider these various points:

Joyful Mysteries: The total openness of the Holy Family to the will of God in all things.

Luminous Mysteries: The selfless love of the Lord Jesus for the Father and humanity throughout his earthly ministry.

Sorrowful Mysteries: The love and compassion poured out by the Lord Jesus and his complete self-immolation for our redemption.

Glorious Mysteries: The open, detached love of Our Lady to the will of God in all things.

Guardian Angel Prayer

Angel of God, my guardian dear,
to whom God's love commits me here,
Ever this day be at my side, to light and
guard, to rule and guide. Amen.

WHEN RELIGION BECOMES SOCIAL ACTIVISM

I will give thanks to the Lord with my whole heart;
I will tell of all thy wonderful deeds.

—Psalm 9:1

Earlier in my life, when I was a high school student and learning how to be a disciple of the Lord Jesus, I participated in a week-long "Christian work" program at a farm organized by local believers. The weekend centered on the biblical practice of gleaning the fields. This was a practice demanded by God in the Old Testament, in which orphans, widows, resident aliens, and the other poor were allowed to go through a farm after harvest and literally "glean" whatever might have been overlooked or missed by the harvesters (see Lev. 19:9–10; Deut. 24:19–21). The practice was an example of God's care for the livelihood of the most vulnerable and the virtue of some of the most powerful.

During the week's experience, we spent long and hot hours in the fields. Early mornings, afternoon breaks, and late evenings were spent in prayer and catechesis. The lessons throughout the experience focused on the biblical emphasis of service to the weak, the most vulnerable, and those on the periphery. Such teachings took deep root in our young minds and hearts—so much so that idealism crept in. We started thinking about how we could do more work, get other people involved, and change the world.

The catechists allowed us to have these types of conversations . . . for a while. Eventually, they stepped in and began to apply some of the biblical wisdom that was being taught to us. On one occasion, one of the female catechists told us, "Remember, our goal is not to change the world. Only God can do that. Our task is to serve the people in front of us, those who are in our area." When we pushed back and insisted that we could do more, she accepted our words, responding, "Yes, please do more, but just make sure that you're serving Jesus Christ. Our task is not to fight the poverty of the world, or to solve every social ill in our world. Our simple task is to be the hands and feet of Christ. We are called to live his poverty of spirit and to humbly do what we can for those in front of us."

This application of biblical wisdom caused quite a stir. We mistakenly thought the woman was a defeatist and lacked the necessary vigor to really fight the evils of our world.

This became a big talking point during the work sessions, and eventually, another catechist came forward. He was a native Spanish-speaker who seemed to be an introvert, but he had some things he wanted to say, and his English was loud and clear. In fact, for young minds, his accent added credibility to his comments.

And so, the gentleman started by summarizing some of the things he had overheard us saying, since we were teenagers and overly loud and inattentive to the adult ears listening to our conversations. After repeating a few of our comments, the catechist said to us, "Remember, this is the Lord's work. We don't steal it and make it into our work. We have to keep Jesus' spirit. This means that we must pray and study the Bible. Our work isn't just in the fields. It's also in our hearts. If we don't work on our hearts, then we only have food for people's bellies. But people need more than that. They need something for their hearts. They need Jesus. And if we give them Jesus, then they can turn around and be Jesus for others."

The portion of that conversation that I've given here is burned into my mind. The force of this catechist's message made a powerful impression on me (and my friends), and it has influenced my understanding of how to fulfill our Christian call to *serve the Lord* in the poor and those in need.

This experience, and its accompanying catechesis, raises some questions. Does the virtue of religion contain a call to serve the poor? If so, what does that look like? How is service to the poor related to worship?

> "I will not allow myself to be so absorbed in the whirlwind of work as to forget about God. I will spend all my free moments at the feet of the Master hidden in the Blessed Sacrament."
>
> —ST. FAUSTINA

Christian Orthopraxy

The entire public ministry of the Lord Jesus was marked by a total dedication to the Father and a profound and attentive service to the sick, poor, vulnerable, and weak. He called his disciples to follow after him, to worship the Father, and to be a consolation to the suffering and a source of hope to the forgotten.

The Lord summarized this twofold summons in response to a question posed to him:

Teacher, which is the great commandment in the law?

And the Lord responded:

You shall love the Lord your God with all your heart, and with all your soul, and with all your mind. This is the great and first commandment. And a second is like it, You shall love your neighbor as yourself (Matt. 22:37–39).

The virtue of religion begins with a true worship of God, but it certainly involves a call to the poor and to those in need. Any person of strong virtue realizes the heartfelt connection between the worship of God and service to the poor and needy.

In imitation of Jesus Christ, and in fulfillment of our human vocation and the moral law, everyone is called to provide help and assistance—as he is able—to the poor and vulnerable.

As St. John fittingly explains:

We love, because he first loved us. If any one says, "I love God," and hates his brother, he is a liar; for he who does not love his brother whom he has seen, cannot love God whom he has not seen (1 John 4:19–20).

Such service to the poor and those in need is called *orthopraxy* in theology. The word means "right action." And so, our outreach to those in need is called to be precisely that, right action, meaning that such service must always be within the bounds of right worship and doctrine. This means we can never remove God from our outreach, diminish his presence, flout or compromise his moral teachings, or seek simply to fill someone's belly without also seeking to fill his heart with the good news.

The two Great Commandments—love of God and neighbor—cannot be separated. If they are divided, then our outreach ceases to be orthodoxy and instead becomes a secularized philanthropy or social service. Such service, though perhaps beneficial in the natural order, bears no supernatural merit for either the ones serving or those receiving the service.

An example will help us to develop a God-centered service to others. In the plethora of stories surrounding St. Teresa of Calcutta, there is one story that accentuates orthopraxy.

Once, while Mother Teresa was washing the body of a dying woman, the woman asked Mother Teresa why she was washing her. The woman was an untouchable in the Indian caste system and did not understand the act of kindness. Mother Teresa told the woman that she washed her because her God had sent her to the woman. But the woman told Mother Teresa that she was a Hindu and worshipped over four hundred gods. Which god did Mother represent?

The woman told Mother that she did not know her God. Mother replied that on the contrary, she did. The woman again told Mother that she did not know her God and did not understand why she was with her and washing her.

Mother Teresa gently answered the woman: "You know my God. My God is love, and he has called me to be here with you."

The encounter shows us the central importance of a theological worldview whenever we serve others. The call for orthopraxy raises a couple of questions. How do the worship of God and outreach to the poor and those in need complement each other? How are we to understand and live their connection within the virtue of religion?

> "You can find Calcutta anywhere in the world. You only need two eyes to see. Everywhere in the world there are people that are not loved, people that are not wanted nor desired, people that no one will help, people that are pushed away or forgotten. And this is the greatest poverty."
>
> —ST. TERESA OF CALCUTTA

Worship and Service

The virtue of religion is first and foremost about the worship of the living God. Flowing from this worship, there is born a love for neighbor. The Lord Jesus teaches us that the virtue of religion involves the delicate balance between a love of the Father and a love of our neighbor. The Lord Jesus, and the early Church, modeled this way of life for us.

Two events from the life of the Lord Jesus help us to understand the balance between the worship of God and service to our neighbors.

During the Lord Jesus' great Sermon on the Mount, he emphasized the necessary moral purity for true worship. He tells us:

So if you are offering your gift at the altar, and there remember that your brother has something against you, leave your gift there before the altar and go; first be reconciled to your brother, and then come and offer your gift (Matt. 5:23–24).

This account displays the internal spiritual relationship between worship and service. It emphasizes the dynamics between a love of our neighbor and the adoration of God. The Lord stresses that we cannot love and worship God in spirit and truth unless we are without fault toward our neighbor. This is true about those with whom we might have a grievance (or who have grievances against us), and it is also true for those who are in a position of need, especially the poor, the sick, and those on the edge of society.

On another occasion, Jesus was at Bethany in the house of Simon the leper. A woman came to him with an alabaster jar of rich ointment. As a gesture of love, she poured it on his head as he sat at the table.

When the disciples saw it, they were angry.

In reaction, they said, "Why this waste? For this ointment might have been sold for a large sum, and given to the poor." But Jesus said to them, "Why do you trouble the woman? For she has done a beautiful thing to me. For you always have the poor with you, but you will not always have me. In pouring this ointment on my body she has done it to prepare me for burial. Truly, I say to you, wherever this gospel is preached in the whole world, what she has done will be told in memory of her" (Matt. 26:8–13).

This account is significant since it shows the response of the Lord Jesus when the priority of the two Great Commandments is inverted. The love of God must always be our first and primary love. In our fallenness, we need love for God in order to truly love our neighbor, since without a divine love, our love for our neighbors will become adulterated by a sense of quid pro quo, entitlement, self-pity, and exaggerated expectations. When a love of neighbor seeks to upstage the love of God, it must be called out and humbled. When our love for our neighbors, and its accompanying service, is separated from a love of God, it becomes foreign to the way of the gospel and must be disciplined and corrected.

In the account, the apostles are angry that precious oil is being used on the Lord Jesus rather than being sold for the sake of the poor. The Lord hears their words (and knows their thoughts) and admonishes them, since nothing compares to the true worship and adoration of God. Such homage is the beginning of all the other good things that flow from the human heart. In addition, the Lord notes that the poor will always be among us. There is no universal cure for this social ill since it's caused by our fallen nature. Moreover, the greatest service we can give to the poor (or to any neighbor) is a genuine love of God, since such a love brings out our best and helps us to give more selflessly and generously to others.

The balance that is displayed in these two events in the life of the Lord Jesus is also beautifully set forth in the prayer he gave to his apostles (and to us) when they asked him, "Lord, teach us to pray" (Luke 11:1).

Traditionally, there are seven petitions identified in the Lord's Prayer. Likened to the two tablets of the Ten Commandments, with their emphasis on love of God and love of neighbor, the first three petitions of the Lord's Prayer relate to our relationship with God: God's name, God's kingdom, and God's will. The last four petitions of the Lord's Prayer relate to our relationship with our neighbors and the world around us: give us, forgive us, lead us, and deliver us.

The balance between the love of God and the love of neighbor is particularly played out in the middle, central petition of the prayer—namely, "give us this day our daily bread."

Since many of us have prayed this prayer since we were children, we can overlook the obvious redundancy. Why do we ask twice for bread in this one petition: "this day['s bread]" and "daily bread"?

The early Church explored the depth of the Lord's Prayer, and we still benefit from its prayerful discernment. The early teachers of our faith are almost unanimous in the opinion that the two references to bread are indications of both earthly food ("this day") and supernatural food ("daily")—namely, to the food of the earth that we need for our sustenance and to the eucharistic food that is needed for eternal salvation.

The inclusion of the earthly and supernatural breads into the heart of the Lord's Prayer is an eminently practical double-emphasis of the Great Commandments, to love God and our neighbor. If we neglect one, or separate them, or deprioritize them, then we will suffer a malnutrition of our personhood and will lack the needed strength to live abundantly. The two must accompany each other, in their proper order, for us to grow and prosper as human beings and as children of God.

This point is further made in the *Catechism of the Catholic Church*. In describing the spiritual benefits of receiving Holy Communion in a worthy manner, the *Catechism* teaches that a good Communion "commits us to the poor." By receiving the body and blood of Jesus Christ, "given up for us," we are given the grace to recognize the Lord in the poorest among us, who are truly his brothers and sisters (CCC 1397). Following this teaching, the *Catechism* quotes St. John Chrysostom:

You have tasted the blood of the Lord, yet you do not recognize your brother. . . . You dishonor this table when you do not judge worthy of sharing your food someone judged worthy to take part in this meal. . . . God freed you from all your sins and invited you here, but you have not become more merciful.

In our own lives, do we understand the importance of the two Great Commandments and the delicate balance between them? Do we discredit the importance of a true love and a lasting worship of God in a misplaced service to the poor and needy? Do we try to place earthly results and successes above the adoration of God?

> "Let us go forward in peace, our eyes upon heaven, the only one goal of our labors."
> —ST. THÉRÈSE OF LISIEUX

The Unity of the Spirit

In the Old Testament, we're told the peculiar story of Moses and the rock (Num. 20:1–13). In the account, God's people are in the desert after their liberation from Egypt. They are bemoaning the lack of water, even saying to Moses: "And why have you made us come up out of Egypt, to bring us to this evil place? It is no place for grain, or figs, or vines, or pomegranates; and there is no water to drink" (v. 5).

In response, Moses and Aaron go to the tabernacle and ask God for assistance. It is a powerful witness that the servants of God turn to prayer and the tent of worship in seeking an answer. God answers their prayers and tells Moses to go and talk to the rock, commanding it to bear water (v. 8). The instruction is simple but awkward. Did God really command his servant Moses to talk to a rock?

God truly spoke such a directive, and he relied on Moses to trust and obey him. Even though Moses could not imagine how such an odd request could solve the problems of the people, God expected Moses to surrender to him and do as he was instructed.

Moses, however, did not obey. With Aaron, he assembled the people before the rock and exhorted them, saying: "Hear now, you rebels; shall we bring forth water for you out of this rock?" (v. 10). And then, relying on his own counsel and ingenuity, Moses lifted up his hand and struck the rock twice with his staff (v. 11). Although this made practical sense to him, it was not what God had commanded. Yet, in response to Moses' actions, water came out abundantly, and the congregation and their livestock drank.

Due to this lack of faith, Moses lost the opportunity to enter the promised land. God spoke to Moses, saying: "Because you did not believe in me, to sanctify me in the eyes of the people of Israel, therefore you shall not bring this assembly into the land which I have given them" (v. 12).

It's important to note that God had something else planned, something even greater than Moses could have imagined, since he said "to show my holiness." If Moses had obeyed, then God would have worked a far mightier work before the eyes of his people. But Moses trusted only himself and his own reasoning and his own state of affairs. Because of this short-sightedness and narrow-mindedness, the greater signs of God could not be done. In addition, Moses would not be permitted to enter the land of his forefathers.

Because you broke faith with me in the midst of the people of Israel at the waters of Mer'i-bath-ka'desh, in the wilderness of Zin; because you did not revere me as holy in the midst of the people of Israel. For you shall see the land before you; but you shall not go there, into the land which I give to the people of Israel (Deut. 32:51–52).

It is significant that Moses' disobedience still brought about earthly success. As he struck the rock, water came forth, and the Israelites and their livestock drank freely. From the consensus of the people, Moses was a real hero. The truth, however, was that he himself was a rebel, even as he accused the Israelites of such an offense. In addition, he deprived God's people of an even greater sign, which will be forever unknown.

The above account is highly symbolic for all God's people. It is particularly provocative for the person or group who knows right doctrine, and the moral truth that flows from it, yet dismisses them for a personal judgment, an earthly state of affairs, or a conclusion reached through ideology. As in the account, such persons or groups are called to trust and to do what the Lord commands, even if right doctrine and moral truth might appear as peculiar as talking to a rock. God calls for faith. He relies on obedience in order to care for his people and to show his holiness.

As with Moses, such people or groups might find worldly success. Such achievements, however, are not the litmus test of moral fulfillment. Earthly accomplishment is never a sign of moral goodness or spiritual righteousness. In fact, such successes—born from rebellion—come at a high price. The disobedience that motivates such wayward actions could bar the people involved in them from our eternal homeland.

Such faithlessness of leadership only frustrates the broader plan of God to provide and care for his people.

And so, the group or person who wants to turn religion into social activism should beware. The work of God and love for our neighbors cannot ever be separated from the love of God and an obedience to his commands. All the actions of a believer should be solely motivated by the supernatural, moral-spiritual worldview that's born from living out the twofold commandments to love God and our neighbor. Worldly success, devoid of right doctrine and moral truth, is no success at all. It pre-empts and rejects God's divine Providence, and so brings a terrible spiritual and moral loss.

Such offenses can be seen by supposed believers and "Catholic" organizations that counsel married couples to use contraception, unwed mothers to pursue abortion, young people to "carry a condom," environmentalists to discard human dignity and the basic needs of human life, activists to violate justice for corrupt race theories, and so many other social situations in which the wisdom of God, and that of the Church, is discarded for the pretend wisdom of our age, ideology, or human machination.

The early Church displayed its unity by shared worship, prayer, doctrine, community life, and service to the poor (see Acts 2:42). When doctrine is broken, the unity of the community is threatened. In response, St. Paul admonishes:

> I therefore, a prisoner in the Lord, beg you to lead a life worthy of the calling to which you have been called, with

all lowliness and meekness, with patience, forbearing one another in love, eager to maintain the unity of the Spirit in the bond of peace. There is one body and one Spirit, just as you were called to the one hope that belongs to your call, one Lord, one faith, one baptism, one God and Father of us all, who is above all and through all and in all (Eph. 4:1–6).

The apostle to the Gentiles exhorts us to keep "the unity of the Spirit." However much we might be tempted by social activism and the successes of this world, we must remain faithful and preserve "the bond of peace" with the community of believers, especially its shepherds.

As such, those social reformers and political activists who betray the Faith, and divide the Great Commandments, must be called out and held accountable. They must realize the harm they are doing to right doctrine and moral truth.

In our discipleship, do we trust God enough to obey him even when we think something else will be more successful? Are we willing to die to worldly wisdom so that God can manifest his holiness and the love he has for his people? Do we preserve the unity between the love of God and our neighbor?

> "Allow the light and the healing presence of Christ to shine brightly through your lives. In that way, all those who come in contact with you will discover the loving kindness of God."
>
> —POPE ST. JOHN PAUL II

Criteria of the Virtue of Religion

Since we've now explored religion as social activism, let's see how social activism measures up against the five criteria of the true virtue of religion.

1. *God as God:* When religion becomes social activism, people believe they must be God and that they are the ones who must create and move a man-made "providence." There is no room for God and his supernatural worldview.

2. *Humble Recognition:* Social activism as religion is an arrogant, proud movement. It feels disappointed by God and is critical of any recognition of him. Activism tends to nurture rage toward God and anyone who opposes it.

3. *Debt to God:* Social activism as religion is offended by any reference to a "debt" to God, since it is convinced that God has failed and must "make up" for failures.

4. *Gratitude and Obedience:* When religion becomes social activism, there is no gratitude to anyone, only entitlement and rage. There is no obedience to a moral truth above it, since social activism deludes itself into thinking its perspective is the only true law.

5. *Connection to Others:* For all of its interaction in society and among people in supposed service, there is actually very little connection with others. Social activism as religion looks upon people as numbers and statistics. Any personal connection is lost.

In the above assessment, we see the dangers and tragedies that occur when religion becomes self-activism. In recognizing such dangers, we need to examine when and how such overtures have entered into our own exercise of the virtue of religion. The following *Application to Our Own Lives* will assist us in this review.

Application to Our Lives

Examination of conscience

The following questions are meant as a help in examining our own consciences on the virtue of religion and the worship of God:

- Do I approach God with suspicion?

- Do I think God has failed in his care of his people?

- Do I think I can do better than God in caring for his people?

- Have I kept the unity between love of God and neighbor?

- Do I seek to selflessly serve my neighbor?

- Do I go the extra mile in service, even to those people I don't like?

- Have I neglected the power of worship and prayer in my service to others?

- Have I fed the bellies of my neighbors but ignored their hearts?

- Have I participated in a group or outreach that disobeys right doctrine or moral truth?

- Do I regularly praise God for the beauty and mystery of his divine Providence?

Having made this examination of conscience, it is recommended that you go and make a good confession based on these points.

Pointers for apologetics

As a help in speaking to our fellow believers or to unbelievers around us, here are some pointers for apologetics:

1. God is the Lord of all things. His Providence is both mysterious and powerful.

2. In order for God's holiness and goodness to be seen, his children must trust and obey him.

3. When religion becomes social activism, there is a denial of God's Providence and a dividing of the two Great Commandments to love God and our neighbor.

4. Social activism deludes itself and accepts pretend worldly wisdom over and above the wisdom and power of God.

5. True Christian service relies on right doctrine, moral truth, and true religion.

Key points

Having the pointers for apologetics as a foundation, we can now stress some key points from this chapter:

- Social activism is a rebellion against the Providence of God. It is an arrogant and proud spirit.

- Social activism attempts to take over the action and care of God for his people.

- The life of the Lord Jesus and that of the early Church, as well as the two Great Commandments, give clear catechesis on the unity among right doctrine, moral truth, and social outreach.

- The fourth petition of the Lord's Prayer references both earthly and supernatural bread. This twofold indication shows the unity of serving both the material and spiritual well-being of our neighbors.

- No believer or Catholic organization can justify a break from right doctrine for the empty promise of earthly success.

Devotional exercise

Peace Prayer of St. Francis of Assisi
Lord, make me an instrument of your peace;
Where there is hatred, let me sow love;
Where there is injury, pardon;
Where there is error, truth;
Where there is doubt, faith;

Where there is despair, hope;
Where there is darkness, light;
And where there is sadness, joy.

O Divine Master,
Grant that I may not so much seek
To be consoled, as to console;
To be understood, as to understand;
To be loved as to love.
For it is in giving that we receive;
It is in pardoning that we are pardoned;
And it is in dying that we are born to eternal life.
Amen.

The Lord's Prayer
Our Father, who art in heaven,
hallowed be thy name.
Thy kingdom come,
thy will be done on earth, as it is in heaven.
Give us this day our daily bread
and forgive us our trespasses,
as we forgive those who trespass against us;
and lead us not into temptation,
but deliver us from evil.
Amen.

Act of Faith
O my God, I firmly believe

that you are one God in three divine Persons,
Father, Son, and Holy Spirit.
I believe that your divine Son became man
and died for our sins and that he will come
to judge the living and the dead.
I believe these and all the truths
which the Holy Catholic Church teaches
because you have revealed them
who are eternal truth and wisdom,
who can neither deceive nor be deceived.
In this faith I intend to live and die.
Amen.

Stations of the Cross

As you pray the stations of the cross,
ask for the graces to avoid the virtue
of religion becoming social activism. In
particular, focus on the *second station* when
Jesus accepts his cross: "So they took Jesus,
and he went out, bearing his own cross,
to the place called the place of a skull,
which is called in Hebrew Gol'gotha."

—JOHN 19:17

Rosary Suggestions

When praying the mysteries of the rosary, consider these various points:

Joyful Mysteries: The connection between the works of the Holy Family and their total trust in the ways of God.

Luminous Mysteries: The way of the Lord Jesus in loving the Father while preaching and doing the works of the kingdom.

Sorrowful Mysteries: The communion between the love of Jesus for the Father and the saving works of his passion and death.

Glorious Mysteries: The splendor that awaits all men and women who cooperate with God's grace and who both love and serve him in all things.

Guardian Angel Prayer

Angel of God, my guardian dear,
to whom God's love commits me here,
Ever this day be at my side, to light
and guard, to rule and guide. Amen.

CONCLUSION

Several years ago, there was a death, and a family wished to meet and talk with the priest who would be celebrating the funeral Mass. I was helping at the parish, and the pastor asked if I could take the funeral and assist with the pastoral needs of the grieving family. I was happy to assist and looked forward to seeing how I could help.

When the time came, the family and I sat down and began to discuss their loved one's life and accomplishments. I took a few notes. Then we moved into the selection of Scripture readings. There were some clarifying questions, but everything seemed well. Then we began to address the music.

The family asked if they could have a beloved secular song at the funeral. I explained that only approved liturgical music could be sung but that such a display of affection could be done among the family the night before. They weren't happy with the answer, and they pushed back, saying, "Father, this would mean a great deal to our family." I acknowledged the sentiment but indicated that such secular music would be inappropriate for such a sacred event.

They weren't pleased, but we moved on. They asked if we could have a eulogy. I indicated that eulogies are discouraged, but one could be offered so long as it focused on the paschal mystery, which I had to explain to them. They were confused and told me they wanted to list all the things their loved one had achieved in his life. I again mentioned that such an account of personal achievements and self-help could be described and listed among the family. It has its place, but not in the funeral Mass.

At this point, the family became frustrated and asked if another priest was available. When I indicated that the pastor was planning to be away and that my guidance was according to his parish policies (not to mention the liturgical law of the Church), they threatened to go to another parish. I indicated that they could pursue such options and that I would be happy to make a few phone calls on their behalf. My sincere efforts to help them in this moment of commodity were not appreciated.

Finally, they calmed down. I remained calm throughout the meeting and attempted to approach them with the gentleness and compassion that should be given to any grieving family.

But they had one more request. Their loved one had served on the board of a local outreach organization, and the organization wanted to present him with a posthumous award. The family thought it would be wonderful to do it at the funeral. Again, and not trying to be the bad guy, I explained that such social activism is noble, but such awards would not be appropriate in the funeral Mass. I suggested that perhaps the award could be given at the graveside service or at the reception afterward.

At this counsel, the family blew up. They were irate and beside themselves. Knowing that the apparent issues are never *the* issues and that people grieve in different ways, including via anger, I waited, and when they were relatively calm, I asked if I could talk with them about what the funeral Mass truly is and what we get to participate in during its celebration.

They were not overly thrilled with my request, but they were somewhat compliant. And so, using a softened voice, I dove right in.

"The funeral Mass is when we offer fitting adoration to God. We pray and lift up supplication for the eternal repose of your loved one's soul. This is done during a Mass so that the re-presentation of the sacrifice of the Lord Jesus, to the Father, by the power of the Holy Spirit, will be offered for his eternal rest. We don't 'personalize' the Mass since it belongs to the Lord Jesus and his full mystical body throughout the ages. We don't have to 'make it special' with sentiment, self-help, or social activism.

"The Funeral Mass is already eternally special and of immense spiritual power. You don't have to rely on commodity to find the best deal among different priests or parishes, since the best gift that your loved one will be given is by the Lord Jesus himself, as he offers this sacrifice for your loved one and seeks to be the Good Shepherd by purging him of any venial sins and temporal punishment so that he can be presented to the Father in all his glory and majesty."

After I was done, the family were speechless. They asked me, "And all that is real?"

Suppressing a smile, I nodded and declared to them: "Yes, this is the reality. This is all real."

The conversation continued, but with a much deeper spiritual focus. In many respects, by seeing a renewed glimpse of the glory that awaits those who love God, this family realized what Job described when he exclaimed:

I had heard of thee by the hearing of the ear, but now my eye sees thee (Job 42:5).

There is also what St. Paul experienced when Ananias laid hands upon him, as recounted in the Acts of the Apostles:

So Anani'as went and entered the house. And laying his hands on him he said, "Brother Saul, the Lord Jesus who appeared to you on the road by which you came, has sent me that you may regain your sight and be filled with the Holy Spirit." And immediately something like scales fell from his eyes and he regained his sight (9:17–18).

The conversion that happened in this family is the greater conversion that we need among all believers today. We need a deeper spiritual awareness that God, his providential plan, his economy of salvation, and his call for us to worship him are all true and real and merit the response of our entire life.

The conversation above could have happened in any parish in the universal Church. It could occur with almost every family, or portions of families, throughout the world.

The virtue of religion has been beaten up, eclipsed, overtaken, and redefined, and its depth of spiritual and moral richness has been needlessly hidden. I pray that this book has reminded us all of the eternal value of worshipping God. I pray that it has reignited a desire to respond to the call to worship and that it has exposed some of its mistaken forms in our culture today. Lastly, I pray that this book has allowed the virtue of religion to shine and call us all back to greater and more heartfelt worship.

Our Time Together

Throughout this book, the effort has been made to unmask some of the many threats to true religion. We walked through the challenges posed by sentiment, self-help, commodity, and social activism. Certainly, there are other threats, but in my priestly ministry, I have found these four to be the most pressing.

I pray that the review of each challenge to the virtue of religion has been helpful to you in understanding and appreciating the strength and vitality of this important virtue. I further hope that the application section of each chapter has given you some insights and talking points on each topic, as well as a blueprint for a spiritual response to each of these threats in your own spiritual life and the lives of your loved ones.

As you conclude this book, I encourage you to flip back to the front and possibly re-read chapter one and its exposition on the positive elements and spiritual benefits of the virtue of religion.

Thank you for reading this book. Please consider passing it along to someone who might be encouraged by it—a family member, friend, co-worker, or neighbor.

In the spirit of true religion, I conclude with the blessing of Moses to Aaron (Num. 6:24–26):

The Lord bless you and keep you:
the Lord make his face to shine upon you,
and be gracious to you:
the Lord lift up his countenance upon you,
and give you peace.

Amen.

BIBLIOGRAPHY

General Sources:

Bible. Revised Standard Version Catholic Edition.
Catechism of the Catholic Church. Vatican City State.

Specific Sources:

Aquinas, Thomas. *Summa Theologica.* Second Revised
Edition. Fathers of the English Dominican Province.

Augustine. *City of God.* Trans. Henry Bettenson. New
York: Penguin Books, 1984.

Cicero. *The Nature of the Gods.* Trans. H. Rackman.
Cambridge: Harvard University Press, 1979.

Hahn, Scott. *A Father Who Keeps His Promises: God's
Covenant Love in Scripture.* Pomona: Servant, 1998.

John Paul II. Encyclical *Redemptor Hominis.* 1979.

Kereszty, Roch A. *Wedding Feast of the Lamb: Eucharistic
Theology from a Biblical, Historical, Systematic Perspective.*
Chicago: Hillenbrand Books, 2004.

Kirby, Jeffrey. *Thy Kingdom Come: Living the Lord's Prayer in
Everyday Life.* Charlotte: TAN Books, 2019.

Pitre, Brant. *Jesus and the Jewish Roots of the Eucharist*. New York: Doubleday, 2011.

Royal, Robert. *The God That Did Not Fail: How Religion Built and Sustains the West*. New York: Encounter Books, 2010.

About the Author

Father Jeffrey Kirby, S.T.D., is the Pastor of Our Lady of Grace Parish in Indian Land, South Carolina. He holds a doctorate in moral theology from the Holy Cross University in Rome and serves as an adjunct professor of Theology at Belmont Abbey College. He is the author of several books, including *Way of the Cross for Loved Ones Who Have Left the Faith.*